Hargrave Jennings

The Indian Religions

Results of the mysterious Buddhism, concerning that also which is to be

understood in the divinity of fire

Hargrave Jennings

The Indian Religions
Results of the mysterious Buddhism, concerning that also which is to be understood in the divinity of fire

ISBN/EAN: 9783337235581

Printed in Europe, USA, Canada, Australia, Japan

Cover: Foto ©Lupo / pixelio.de

More available books at **www.hansebooks.com**

THE INDIAN RELIGIONS

OR

RESULTS OF THE MYSTERIOUS

BUDDHISM

CONCERNING THAT ALSO WHICH IS TO BE UNDERSTOOD IN THE DIVINITY OF FIRE.

BY

HARGRAVE JENNINGS

AUTHOR OF "THE ROSICRUCIANS: THEIR RITES AND MYSTERIES,"
"PHALLICISM: ITS CONNECTION WITH THE ROSICRUCIANS AND THE
GNOSTICS AND ITS FOUNDATION IN BUDDHISM," &c., &c.

LONDON
GEORGE REDWAY
YORK STREET COVENT GARDEN
1890.

ANALYSIS OF CONTENTS.

PREFACE.

Two things the Author must premise in relation to the following book. In the first place, the Philosophical Results attained in this volume stand as the persuasions of years of much research, and of a great amount of thought. This upon subjects which must ever, in the nature of things, surmount and exceed all others in importance. In the business of the world, student-thought is not valued. In the activity of the world, student-work is ignored. It is only in its calm regards to the future—at the rarest times—that Civilisation, and especially our Modern Hyper-Civilisation, grows grave in its reflections on what Human Nature should mean:—of what the destinies of our "Mysterious Race" should be. What they should really be.

In the second place, the Author desires that a wide interval of consideration should be allowed between the original religion of the Hindoos—ancient beyond count—and the writer's acceptation of its sublime philosophical groundwork, and the modern practice of the Indian beliefs, deformed as

they have become, in the course of the centuries—
indeed, as all religions become as time advances with
them—by forms more or less mechanical, and by
superstition, in the greater, or lesser degree, gross
—that is, humanly gross. It is the fact that the
mere Man-View of their essence, of their solemnities,
and of their character, constitutes creeds. The modern
Indian religions—are religions. In short, are Codes.
Codes fitted to the Peoples.

Treating as this work humbly does upon matters
the most abstruse that can occupy the mind of the
Thinker, and involving as the perusal of this book
necessarily must the power of the seizure of pure
abstractions, the author need not say that, as he is
only seeking to render distinct, and to clearly expound,
the opinions of some of the greatest of men, his book
is not to be judged lightly. In fact, it is a treatise
specially addressed to Thinkers, and to them alone.

THE INDIAN RELIGIONS;

OR,

Results of the Mysterious Buddhism.

———◆◆◆———

CHAPTER I.

BUDDHISM THE FOUNDATION OF ALL THE RELIGIONS OF INDIA.

BUDDHISM, which, with its truths, underlies all the religious beliefs of the vast East, and which, though free of all the ceremonial and the forms which always spread and figure in every faith when it has tran-scended through its philosophical and thinking ele-ment and passed to man, or rather when it has de-scended and seeks man through his investitures, undoubtedly was the origin of the modern Brah-minical religion.

This faith is pre-eminently mystical, and therefore metaphysical. It starts with that conclusion of all sound and *exhausted* metaphysics, that the world—rightly looked at—is a compromise; that everything which is perceived outwardly or thought inwardly, to be perceived or thought at all, must be concrete and pass under the laws of apprehension, which are *forms*; and that forms are unreal, inasmuch as they are acci-

B

dents.   That cannot be true that requires something
else to make it true.

The seeker after knowledge will transcend all
spheres until he arrives at that beyond which nothing
supposable can be.   Looking upon life, in its totality,
as being impossible without concentred identity, and
concluding that life was inconceivable apart from
form, oneness, or number (the doctrine of unity of
Pythagoras, mistaken as that of *number* by Aristotle
and others) ; the Buddhists pronounced that life and
its shows—including the whole universe—was a
phantasm existing only in the mind conceiving it;
which mind—the thing perceived being necessary,
and real of it, and making it mind, and in fact being
it, modified only by that surrounding for the purpose
of finding itself—was alone all.   This is the pure
immateriality of the Berkeleyan theory, which, penetrating across the procession of images which make
life that which we find it, and the sole coherence and
existence of which life, perhaps, depends upon the
uninterrupted introduction of *ideas* which we deno-
minate remembrance, sense of unity, or identity of
self; this passes out into the void beyond, in which
it is evaporate, having nothing—nothing of form—of
which to sustain.   Hume, and the sceptics, who denied
knowledge and the possibility of knowledge, contending simply for the acceptance of these delusions
as alone possible for man ; in the great demonstration
of the philosophically unreal union and bond of
" cause and effect," adopted, without knowing it, the
old Buddhist doctrine of coverings and investitures or
ideas, *as men alone,* without reference to aught outside :

in which coverings and investitures man's knowledge—nay, man *himself*—alone lay.

Considering that everything conceivable was base and low, a necessary deceit for man to be possible; and forms, as coming out of matter, including that form or process, the mind of man, or *men*, was mere arbitrary vapour, or as signs accepted by the mind conceiving them as a step or rest to return in upon itself and find itself—the Buddhist rejected the whole visible world, and abandoned the human being as a machine necessary only because, to be at all, it must be as it is. This is the *Nirvaná*, or nothingness, so mistaken for atheism by incompetent and modern reviewers of Buddhism.

The truth is, that it is not atheism at all, but the proper following out and the logical search down to its basis of all consistent and believable philosophy. It is the rigid mathematical demonstrations of Spinoza carried out and summed. It is the conclusion and result of Hobbes' search—and vain search—for soul in the relics—self-moved—of the senses. It is the "form," or "number," or "show" of Pythagoras. It is the Emptied Heaven of the Platonists. It is the exhausted dream-world of the mystics; the quietism of the Quakers; the one ultimate "mind-emptying-out" of all philosophers, and of all the hypernaturally laborious systems of which philosophy—or the *getting behind nature*—is capable. And this is that which the vain talkers of that which they do not understand stigmatise as atheism. Rather it is making God all, including we, ourselves, by totally annihilating matter, and deriding it as a fiction and an impossibility.

Of all matter of inquest, the refined speculations of the Buddhists have been the most reluctant to submission. And yet, without mastering these abstractions, no religion of the East can be really understood. That the Orientals have deep grounds for their beliefs, no one who has penetrated, however slightly, into the mysteries of their faiths could have failed to discover. Very erroneous notions are entertained even among philosophers—much more among theologians—as to what is really meant by Buddhism. But a volume alone could be written on this head, and, in the above, we have only given a hint of what the sages of the East believed, and supplied a specimen of the extraordinarily close manner in which they argued upon these evading and subtle themes.

CHAPTER II.

HISTORICAL DESCRIPTION OF THE RELIGIONS OF INDIA AND OF THE EAST.

WE will now supply the reader with a concise description of the various principal religions believed in Asia. We will commence with Brahmanism, and rise to Buddhism, from which latter, indeed, the religion of Brahma derives its origin. Brahmanism is the world-adaptation of the great—otherwise incomprehensible—elements of Buddhism to states and peoples.

Brahmanism acknowledges *Para Brahma* as the Supreme God; but this god does not act, he delegates his power to Brama, Vishnu, Siva, and a multitude of subaltern deities assigned for the government of the world. Brama rules the earth, Vishnu the water, and Siva the fire. These three persons are, nevertheless, but one God, and they form the *Indian Trinity*, called *Trimour tree.*

The Hindoos, who profess this religion, have several sacred books, named *Vedas.* They are written in Sanscrit, and form their religious and philosophical code. They admit the metempsychosis, and, in consequence of this belief, certain classes abstain from the flesh of all kinds of animals. Brahmanism commands the moderating of the passions, and teaches the immortality of the soul, its purification by penance and voluntary abstinence, and a vast number of religious practices.

All the members of this religion, which extends nearly throughout India, have, from the remotest times, been divided into four castes, all intermixture of which is forbidden. Those castes are, the *Brahmins*, who are the learned and the priests, and form the class from which all public functionaries are taken; the *Cshatryas*, or Kettris, destined to the military profession; it is from them that sprang the Rajahs, who established the principalities of once independent India; the *Nairs* of the Deccan are connected with it.

The *Vaishyas*, or *Beizes*, are devoted to agriculture, cattle-breeding, and dealing in the produce of the soil, and manufactured articles; those who occupy themselves in commerce, especially in foreign countries, are styled *Banians*; a great number of the Mahrattas belong to this class. The *Sudras*, or *Tshutri*, are the artisans and labourers. Each of these four principal castes is subdivided into several secondary. Among the Hindoos, the descendants of those who, by unlawful marriages, have derogated from the rights of the leading castes, are comprised in the ignoble and despised division, called *Varná-Sankara*. Still lower than these mixed or bastard castes we find the unfortunate *Parias*. These beings are obliged to live in solitary places, to shun the sight of a Hindoo, to distinguish their wells by a circle of animals' bones, and to employ themselves in the most disgusting occupations. On the other hand they may eat everything.

The Brahmanic worship is accompanied by a great number of ceremonies and solemn usages. Some of them are horrible; such is the procession of the god Juggernaut, beneath the wheels of whose ponderous car fanatics throw themselves to be crushed, in the belief that they are thus gaining the most glorious of deaths and eternal happiness.

There are other festivals, in which reign tumult and licentiousness; where the shameless *Lingam* is shown to the prostrated multitude. Ablutions and lustrations make a prominent part of the Brahminical worship; the images of the divinities are solemnly washed in the rivers and lakes. Several rivers, among which are the Ganges, the Nerbudda, and the Kristna, are held sacred. There are many places to which the Hindoos make pilgrimages; the most celebrated and frequented are stated by Mr. Hamilton to be Juggernaut, Benares, Gaza, Allahabad, Tripaty, Dwaraca, Somnath, Ramisseram, the Maransoar Lake, Gangoutri, Joalamukhi, Omercuntuc, Trimbaka-Nasser, Pervatam, Parkar, Madura, and Bindrabund.

The barbarous custom of the women of the first two castes, who immolate themselves on the funeral piles of their husbands, is a remnant of the human sacrifices which were anciently very frequent. Even in latter times, during epidemics and public calamities, Brahmins have been seen to throw themselves from the summit of a tower as an expiatory offering.

The Hindoos have numerous temples named *Pagodas*, a word borrowed from the Persian; some of them are exceedingly remarkable for their architecture and their magnitude.

The Hindoos, or, as they are likewise called, Gentoos, have from time immemorial been divided into four great tribes, or castes; which classification is attributed to Menu, the son or grandson of Brahma. To the first and most noble tribe belong the Brahmins, who alone can officiate in the priesthood, like the Levites among the Jews.

The second in order is the Kshatriyas tribe, who, according to their original institution, ought to be all soldiers. But they frequently follow other professions.

The third is the tribe of Vaisyas, who are chiefly merchants, bankers, husbandmen, and shopkeepers.

The fourth tribe is that of Sudra, who ought to be artisans, labourers, or menial servants. If any of them should be excommunicated from any of the four tribes, he and his posterity are for ever shut out from the society of every person in the nation, except that of the Paria or Pariah, who are holden in detestation by all the other tribes, and are employed only in the meanest and vilest offices.

Besides this grand classification, the Hindoos are sub-divided into castes and smaller tribes, and it has been computed that there are eighty-four of these castes. The order of pre-eminence of all the castes, in a particular city or province, is, in general, indisputably decided. The Indian of an inferior caste would think himself highly honoured by adopting the customs of a superior. But the latter would give battle sooner than not vindicate his prerogatives. The man of an inferior caste receives the victuals prepared by a superior caste with respect. But the superior will not partake of a meal which has been prepared by the hands of an inferior caste.

Their marriages are circumscribed by the same

barriers as the rest of their intercourse. And hence, beside the national physiognomy, the members of each caste preserve an air of great resemblance to one another. There are some castes remarkable for their beauty, and others for their ugliness.

The members of each caste generally adhere to the professions of their forefathers ; from one generation to another, the same families have followed one uniform line of life. But though the rule which confines each caste within its own sphere is inflexible in theory, it is not so in practice.

A Brahmin, unable to subsist by his duties, may live by the duty of a soldier. If he cannot get subsistence in either of these employments, he may apply to tillage and attendance upon cattle, or gain a competence by traffic, avoiding certain commodities.

A Kshatriya in distress may subsist by all these means, but he must not have recourse to the highest functions. In seasons of distress a further latitude is given. The practice of medicine and other learned professions—painting, and other arts, work for wages, menial service, alms, and usury—are among the modes of subsistence allowed to the Brahmin and Kshatriya.

A Vaisya, unable to subsist by his own duties, may descend to the servile acts of a Sudra. And a Sudra, not finding employment by waiting on men of the higher classes, may subsist by handicrafts, principally following those mechanical operations, as joinery and masonry, and practical arts, as painting and writing, by following which he may serve men of superior classes. And although a man of a lower class is, in general, restricted from the acts of a higher class, the

Sudra is expressly permitted to become a trader or a husbandman.

Besides the particular occupations assigned to each of the mixed classes, they have the alternative of following that profession which regularly belongs to the class from which they derive their origin on the mother's side. Those, at least, have such an option who are born in the direct order of the classes, as the Mûrdhábhishicta, Ambasht'ha, and others.

The mixed classes are also permitted to subsist by any of the duties of a Sudra; that is, by menial service, by handicrafts, by commerce, or by agriculture. Hence it appears, that almost every occupation, though regularly it be the profession of a particular class, is open to most classes, and that the limitations, far from being rigorous, do, in fact, reserve only one profession, that of the Brahmin, which consists in teaching the Veda, and officiating at religious ceremonies.

To this early division of the people into castes, we may likewise ascribe a striking peculiarity in the state of India—the permanence of its institutions, and the immutability in the manners of its inhabitants.

What now is in India was always there, and is likely still to continue, at least for some considerable time to come. Neither the ferocious violence and illiberal fanaticism of its Mohammedan conquerors, nor the power of its European masters, have effected any considerable alteration. The same distinctions of condition take place, the same arrangements in civil and domestic society remain, the same maxims of religion are venerated, and the same arts and sciences are cultivated.

All the castes acknowledge the Brahmins for their priests, and from them derive their belief of the transmigration of souls; which leads many of them to afflict themselves even at the death of a fly, although it might have been occasioned by inadvertence. But the majority of castes are less scrupulous, and eat, although very sparingly, of both fish and flesh; yet, like the Jews, not of all kinds indifferently. Their diet chiefly consists of rice and vegetables, dressed with ginger, turmeric, and other hot spices, which grow almost spontaneously in their gardens. They deem milk the purest of food, because they think it partakes of some of the properties of the nectar of their gods, and because they esteem the cow itself almost like a divinity.

Buddhism, or the religion of Buddha, appears to have originated in India, about a thousand years before Jesus Christ. We do not yet certainly know whether it is a reformation of Brahminism, or whether, in its actual form, it is not of prior date. Buddhism rejects the division into castes. Its principal dogmas, which have transformed the savage nomadic tribes of Asia into civilised people, and which have made their beneficent influence be felt as far as Siberia, are the same wherever this worship is practised. The hierarchy alone differs in different countries. But this difference must not lead us to consider Buddhism in any other light than as one religion in which no variation exists.

"Buddhism," says Mr. Klaproth, "supposes, like Brahminism, a perpetual series of creations and destructions of the world. This belief, purely meta-

physical, does not admit the existence of a Supreme
Being. He is replaced by Luminous Space, which
contains within itself all the germs of future beings.
But this Luminous Space is not the highest region of
the world. Above it is a third region, which is
eternal and indestructible. It is here that dwells the
Primitive Cause of the destruction of the perishable
world. Existence is regarded by the Buddhists as
the real evil. *For all that exists is without reality*, and
merely a produce of the illusion which deceives the
senses. While all the intellectual parts dispersed
among matters, from the highest luminous region
down to the infernal regions, throw off everything of
matter which they have contracted, become purified,
perfected, and end by uniting, the universal indestructible spirit, which preserves everything for an
incalculable time *at rest*, till the laws of *damata*, or
destiny, render a new creation necessary; from which,
however, are excepted the beings who, by divesting
themselves wholly of matter, are become *Buddhas*,
and remain plunged in the *Nirvaná*, or eternity of
nothingness, the state opposed to that of existence in
matter.

These beings dwell in the indestructible region,
situated beyond the Luminous Space. It is to preserve
the remembrance of the true doctrine, and to render
men capable of following it, that these beatified
persons descend to earth, from time to time, assume a
body, and manifest themselves to men : the chief of
them appear but once.

These only are, strictly speaking, the *Buddhas*,
properly so called. The others, named *Buddhis'-attva*

manifest themselves several times by different incarnations, till they reach the rank of the first, and show
themselves no more on earth.   These perfect beings
exercise an absolute empire over their enemy, which
is matter, and over its seductive forms.   Disposing, as
masters, of *Maya*, or that illusion which cheats the
senses by its metamorphoses, they can, at pleasure,
destroy or make use of it to accomplish the salvation
of the human race.   All the incarnations of the
Buddhas are effected in the following manner :—
Their souls descend in the form of luminous rays, and
take a body under the envelope of *Maya*.   They do
nothing without a special purpose.   Their operations
are never violent.   Nor do they at all shackle the
free will of the inferior beings who are fettered by
matter, and for the salvation of whom they have
descended.

Down to the present time four *Buddhas* have
already appeared.   The last of them was Shakiamuni,
or Gaudama.   A fifth is yet to come before the destruction of the world.   This will be the *Buddha-
Maitri*, or *Maitari*.   The sect of Ceylon and Ultra-
Gangetic India holds, on the contrary, that this incarnation will take place in the year 4457 of our era, an
epoch at which will end the five thousand years which
are to follow the death of Shakiamuni.

According to the Cingalese books, there exists,
relative to the person of the last *Buddha*, a very considerable difference of opinion between the natives of
Ceylon and Ultra-Gangetic India, and the other
sectaries of the same faith.

The Buddhists believe the world to be inhabited

by various classes of beings. They are either *Tshama*, that is to say, reproductions by birth; *roupa*, material or visible gods; or *aroupa*, immaterial or invisible. These beings ascend, by successive transmigrations, from an inferior to a superior rank, according to their good or bad conduct in their previous state, till they finally obtain the beatitude of *Nirvaná*, or non-existence, meaning thereby existence purged entirely from matter, and consequently not subject to the influence of *Maya*, or illusion. Even as all beings quit continually one kind of existence for another, so also are changes undergone by the worlds which they inhabit. Gaudama himself knows not the beginning or the end of this uninterrupted chain of mundane systems. All the beings inhabiting the *loka*, or universe, produced by a series of destructions and renovations, are classed as follows :—

Men, and the local gods called *Nat*, who inspect and judge the human race. They have the good and evil genii for servants. This first class dwells on earth, and in the atmospheric regions, which comprehend Mount Miemmo, and the sixteen heavens of the Deva, placed one above the other, each surpassing that below it in brightness and splendour.

The second class is that of the *roupa*, or visible gods. It occupies the sixteen highest heavens, up to the twenty-second of *Brahma loka*.

In the third abide the immaterial beings who, having been zealous votaries of the doctrine of Buddha, are placed in the four heavens, from the twenty-third to the twenty-seventh. Lastly, the Buddhas reside in the *bon*, or empire which covers all those heavens.

The Thibetan collection of the principal classic books of the ancient Indian Buddhists is called *Gandjur*, and comprises even grammatical and lexicographical works. It consists of 108 volumes. The Thibetans and Mongouls have constructed temples merely for the reception of these sacred volumes. As the worshippers of Buddha believe that prayers to the Divinity may be rendered efficacious by whatever means put in motion (whether by the mouth or by a mechanical agent), there are in their temples a great number of cylinders, which are kept continually turning by a hydraulic wheel. They contain the volumes of the *Gandjur*, the contents of which, agitated in this manner, are believed to exercise a beneficent influence on the well-being of the human race. In great solemnities a circular frame containing 108 lamps, to represent the volumes of the *Gandjur*, is lighted up, and turned in the same direction as the cylinders. The chaplets of the Buddhist priests are also composed of 108 beads.

Buddhism, which originated in Hindoostan, is no longer so widely spread there as it formerly was. The few votaries which it retains in that vast country bear the name of Buddhas, for the belief of the Jains of the Deccan is now a modified Buddhism. The other Hindoos consider Buddha as merely an incarnation of Vishnu. This religion still subsists, in all its purity, in Nepaul, as well as in Thibet. It was carried thither formerly, and likewise into Bukharia. It is still in vigour in Ceylon. Imported from that island into Ultra-Gangetic India, it is professed in the empires of Burmah and Annam; in China, Corea, and Japan, by a considerable portion of the unlettered population. The Buddhists honour Buddha as a Supreme intelligence, manifested in the person of Shakiamuni. The hierarchy established in Thibet, in the thirteenth century, has successively spread its influence over the Mongoul nations, and some Thunguses.

We must take care not to mistake this hierarchy for a branch or modification of Buddhism. The person of the Dalaï-Lama is only considered as an incarnation of a Buddhic divinity, who in all ages has had a predilection for the countries situated north of India. The series of actual Dalaï-Lamas does not commence before the first half of the fifteenth century. They have a regular hierarchy established in Thibet and Mongoulia.

In its institutions and external practices, Buddhism offers a surprising resemblance to the Romish Church. Among the Buddhists we find pontiffs, patriarchs, charged with the spiritual government of provinces, a council of superior priests, who assemble in conclave to elect a pontiff, and whose insignia even bear a great likeness to those of the cardinals of Rome. Among the Buddhists are also convents of monks and nuns, prayers for the dead, auricular confession, the intercession of saints, fasting, kissing the feet, litanies, processions, and lustral water.

Nanekism, or the religion of the Sikhs, was instituted by Nanek, who, according to Mr. Hamilton, was born in 1419, in the province of Lahore, in Hindoostan. It may be regarded as a mixture of Brahmanism and Islamism. It teaches the most thorough deism. The Sikhs adore one God, recognise future rewards and punishments, tolerate all religions, on none of which will they ever enter into a discussion, believe in a secondary incarnation of the divinity, proscribe the worship of images, and abstain from eating pork. These sectaries acknowledge the authenticity of the Indian Vedas, which, and also the Koran, they look upon as divine books. But they assert that the religion of the Hindoos is corrupted by polytheism, and that the adoration of images has led that people astray from the worship of the true God. They regard ablution as one of the principal duties to be performed. Their temples contain no idols, and their prayers are very simple. This religion experienced great reforms under the pontificate of Gouru-Govind, who died in 1707. The Sikhs consider him as a new prophet, and as the founder of their national power. The followers of this religion reject the distinction of castes, are held to be all soldiers, must renounce tobacco, and let their hair and beard grow. A numerous body of religious warriors, named *Akalees*, has the charge of all that relates to worship. There is a kind of baptism, or initiation, which adult sectaries undergo, and to which every individual must submit who wishes to be admitted into this religion. Every one who desires it is received. This faith is professed by the great mass of the population of the Punjaub, and by all Sikhs who are established in other parts of India.

The Doctrine of the Learned, called also the Religion of Confucius, because that celebrated philosopher is considered as its reformer and patriarch, has for its basis a philosophical pantheism, which has been variously interpreted according to the epochs. "It

c

is thought," says M. Abel Remusat, "that, in remote antiquity, the doctrine of the existence of an omnipotent and remunerating deity was not excluded from it. And various passages of Confucius afford reason for believing that it was admitted by the sage himself. But his negligence in inculcating it to his disciples, the vague meaning of the expressions which he employed, and the care which he took to base exclusively his ideas of morality and justice on the principle of love of order, and on a badly-defined conformity with the designs of Heaven and the march of nature, have allowed succeeding philosophers to go astray. So far, indeed, has this been the case that, since the twelfth century of our era, many of them have fallen into absolute Spinozism, and appealing to the authority of their great master have taught a complex system, which consists of materialism, and degenerates into atheism. The merely civil worship paid to the heavens and to the genii of the earth, stars, mountains, and rivers, as well as to the souls of relations, seems in their eyes a social institution of no consequence, or, at least, of which the meaning may be interpreted in various manners. This worship has no images and no priests. Each magistrate practises it within the sphere of his functions, and the emperor himself is its patriarch. Generally all the learned of China, the empire of Annam and Japan, adhere to it, without, however, relinquishing customs borrowed from other forms of worship. They are more superstitious than religious. Conviction has little to do with their conduct. But habit binds them to practices which they themselves ridicule, such as the distinction of lucky or unlucky days, horoscopes, physiognomy, divination, by the lot, &c., &c.

The religion of Sinto is the most ancient of those which prevail in Japan. It bears a great resemblance to mythological naturalism; of which some learned men even believe it to be a branch. It consists in the adoration of a Supreme Being. But it allows of inferior deities, and prescribes the practice of good works, and abstinence from animal food. Its temples, called *Mie*, contain a mirror, to call to mind that, as the defects of the body are faithfully shown in the glass, so the defects of the soul cannot remain hidden from the sight of the divinity. In some of the temples there is a niche which holds the statue of the deity to whom the edifice is dedicated. The simplicity of this religion has been much diminished since the introduction of Buddhism in Japan. It admits of pilgrimages. It has nuns and brotherhoods of various kinds, and of monks; the last of whom, in particular, turn to account the superstition of the people. Though the religion of Sinto is the most ancient in Japan, the Dairis, or emperors of that country, who are regarded as descendants of the gods, have for a long period conformed to the laws of Buddha.

The worship of spirits, or Mythological Naturalism, of Eastern Asia, is considered by its professors as the primitive religion of the most ancient inhabitants of China. It extends to Japan, Corea, among the Thungusians, and Tonquin; where it has taken various forms, and is actually the faith of all that part of the population which has not embraced Buddhism or the principles of Confucius.

This religion has many dogmas in common with the preceding; only it more strongly recognises the individual existence of genii and demons, independent of the parts of nature over which they preside. And this particular belief has degenerated into polytheism and idolatry, through the ignorance of its followers. The priests and priestesses, who are bound to celibacy, practise magic, astrology, necromancy, and a thousand other superstitions. They are called *Tao-sse*, or *doctors of reason*, because that one of their fundamental doctrines which, six centuries before our era, was taught by Lastsen, one of their masters, is that of the existence of the *Primordial Reason*, creator of the world. This is, in fact, the *Logos* of the Platonists.

Brahmanism, according to Malte-Brun, numbers 60,000,000 professors. Graberg and Pinkerton also ascribe to it the same number. Hassel magnifies the total to 111,353,000. Balbi gives 60,000, Malte-Brun and Graberg reckon 150,000,000 as the aggregate of Buddhists. This, however, includes Buddhism and all its branches. Pinkerton gives 180,000,000; Hassel, 315,977,000; Balbi, 170,000,000. All these estimates may be considered as nearly contemporary; as the two oldest, which are those of Malte-Brun and Graberg, go back only to 1810 and 1813. But there must be, always, great doubt in the statistics relative to such subjects.

CHAPTER III.

BRAHMINISM AND TRANSCENDENTAL PHILOSOPHY.

BRAHMINISM may be considered to be the starred and decorated, and the human-marked child of its inexpressibly sublimely descended parent, Buddhism. But consecrate philosophy is no less its original. Its beginning is no less truth. Its foundations are no less solid. Its humanly unexplainable mystic basis is no less supernaturally firm. Its great truth is no less truth. In a word, its philosophy is no less sound. For religions are as the lees, settlings, and *residuum* of philosophy. Forms are the religious food of the peoples. For you can find no aliment for children in abstractions. Matterless space is not for the breath. You must have something grosser than this for human suspiration. You must have things to be thought, for thinkers, and if the thoughts thought are as the dense molecules which you breathe, your thinking shall be as thick.

Gross air is needed for the children of Adam. Palpable air; which is life. Density—thickness—things—lies, must pass through them. The extenuate air is no region for man's lungs. Abstractions are no medium for his mind-sustenance. The atmosphere of organic life must be crowded—else life dies. Man's mind must be filled with illusive somethings—else it cannot be.

It is this setting up of man ;—this conceit which hath no foundation ;—this false and absurd assumption that man's mind must be the arbitrary measure ;—of which we complain. We blindly and doggedly insist that the Christian civilisation must be the only true one. And true to what standard ? If it be true only to the European measure, the white-faced, modern history standard, it is but a limited, presupposed, and accepted truth. It is only as one side of the great polygon. There are other sides ; each as worthy. It is the only seeing with particular eyes, and laughing at one fashion, inasmuch as it doth not quite agree with *our* fashion. Flesh and blood—the fashion of the man—maketh his difference in the sight of things. As well insist upon a knowledge of things through one sense only—build up the universe through one undivided sense. For thinkers have plainly discovered that, in the real sense, there are not several senses. There is but one. And the ordinary set of senses are only the spreading out, in a radius, as in a prism ; which, fanlike, diverges out, as into a set of colours, the one primitive affection or excitement of body—light. Therefore are man's senses but his sub-divided and opened-out conception :—which he opens out, in his man's capacity, as a fan is opened out.

Man's register of heat has a scale below his *zero* and above his vanishing-point of it. His senses are of the confines between this register. This is his nature. But there is heat above as well as cold below, of which he knows nothing. Above and below this " extracted" portion (which, to him, is the whole of nature) is the supernatural. No less a nature to other apprehensions capable of it.   Now his own scale is sometimes broken, and inroad of the supernatural is made to him.   But the fractures close instantly again, and exclude that which temporarily forced them asunder.   So spirit discloses and disappears. Life is *in* spirit.   Life is the meaning of things.   Spirit is the interjection.

Sight, hearing, taste, touch, and feeling, are as the colour of the moral world.   They are the instruments in the hands of consciousness.   But they have nothing else of it.   Colours are the sentiments or affections of the perceiver.   They are not in objects.   They are not out of them.   They are not in the things which man sees. They are not in the seer.   What, and where, are any objects, *per se?*   Take the seer, and the thing seen, away, and you have the nonentity for which the Buddhist combats.   In fact, colours may be the very efflux, decay, and consumption of objects.   A long lasting surface-dissolution in the wearing away of them in light.   The life of objects—otherwise their colours—the very proof of the insubstantiality of things—is evoked out of them through incalculable space.   Things outside yield senses, as the objects themselves cease when the necessity of the illusion of the presence of them is overpast.

This self-exaggeration of the importance of man is, doubtless, ludicrous in the eyes of the greater powers. Quite naturally an animal of four legs, man has only, somehow, got upright.   His very shame confesses it. Only in reiteration of the divine impulse urging on in his finer tissues—machinery won supernaturally out of the unknowable—has he set his face against the stars. The witness of God's lustres hung in the eternal arch. Lights which, in his, beyond expression, contemptible ignorance, and worse than childish self-vaunting, he has at one time fancied but chandeliers to his abode—as hung over his paltriest microcosm. Misusing the small sense, and that *feeling-out* to objects which the supernal Providence permitted him; fostering, fondling, and flattering the word-catching criticism which he has elected into his thoughts of things; building up in his own mind a wretched image of converse with design, purpose, allowance, and weighing of this and that; industriously hiding himself away from the consciousness of his own wretched insufficiency; and piecing, tinkering, and persuading himself of certain philosophic *madnesses*, or systems, or methods of accounting for that before which he felt himself humbled as into his own native dust—almost, in his meanness, beyond, out of, and infinitely below the Divine Knowledge—this wretched creature, forgetting that even his very stars—suns of revolving groups of prodigious worlds—are to Infinity but as the spangles upon nature's universal Imperial purple; or, in the sublimer view, as the dust which drives before Divinity—this thing, then, has even justified, in his unutterable presumption, that magnificent but impious hyperbole which we have somewhere met: "It should seem as if, in his lofty climbing, man would dare from the Heights of Metaphysics, to spy upon God!"

And we undervalue and leave aside our own persuasions that the old truth of these ancient Indian countries is some truth. Accident—of some sort—

has made us masters of the great Indian Continent. Its old institutions have yielded before the newer and fresher prowess. Shadowy antiquity, and world-revered forms, have faded before the pert, latter-day, Portsmouth red of the British military, physical self-affirmation. Bow and spear—nay, matchlock and elephantine ordnance—have gone down before musket and bayonet, the drilled charge, the briskly-handled battery, and the *huzza* from the round, good-humoured faces of the alert British. The practical code, the applied law, have superseded the *formulas* of a creed, and the reveries and dreams of the swarthy statist. Dreams, indeed, have been driven before steel; Brahminism before books—that is, modern books. The scenery is Oriental; the actors European. The light is God's light; the things are brand new, out of man's workshop. Birmah and Birmingham have been welded. But, spite of all this, we never were any other than half-friends with our brown masses of subjects in the East, and our muslinned and over-awed *entertainers*. We had fences for our fields; but we knew not our cattle in them. And in the most English-like Englishman's mind, has always been the idea that the best part of his rule, that his truest title to the Imperial, lay in his Indian princedoms and his mastery over countries steeped in the glow of the (beyond idea) ancient regality.

"Southern Asia, in general, is the seat of awful images and associations. As the cradle of the human race, it would alone have a dim and reverential feeling connected with it. No man can pretend that the wild, barbarous, and capricious superstitions of Africa, or of savage tribes elsewhere, affect him in the way that he is affected by the ancient, monumental, cruel, and elaborate religions of Indostan, &c. The mere antiquity of Asiatic things, of their institutions, histories, modes of faith, &c., is so impressive, that to me," says a celebrated modern author, " the vast age of the race and name overpowers the sense of youth in the individual. Even Englishmen, though not bred in any knowledge of such institutions, cannot but shudder at the mystic sublimity of castes that have flowed apart, and refused to mix, through such immemorial tracks of time; nor can any man fail to be awed by the name of the Ganges or the Euphrates. It contributes much to these feelings, that Southern Asia is, and has been for thousands of years, the part of the earth most swarming with human life—the great *officina gentium*. Man is a weed in those regions. The vast empires, also, into which the enormous population of Asia has always been cast, give a further sublimity to the feelings associated with all Oriental names and images."

CHAPTER IV.

BUDDHISM AND THE FIRE-PHILOSOPHY.

THE learned public—which is a very small public, if public it may be at all called—and the metaphysicians, who, in these latter days, are everywhere so exceedingly scanty as to be numbered upon the fingers, ought to feel much indebted when any of these nobler and higher subjects are discussed.

These are days when the very intensity of science has absolutely passed over into trifling. As civilisation may grow so polished, as that everything, whether good or bad, shall slide off it, so science may grow so perfect—scientific research may grow so elaborate— as that everything shall become *things*.

The subject of Buddhism is the obscurest in the whole round of learned inquisition. This old, and (beyond all measure) the broadest and the sublimest basis of all the religions of the East;—this ancient and really philosophical belief—demands a capacity to grasp abstractions before its principles can be understood. Men who argue from effect to cause—men who apprehend cause at all—that is, cause as gathered from an experience derivable from being;—cannot but fail in attaining to the disclosure of it. Materialism is a constant charge urged upon the Buddhist. In one sense, materialism is correctly assured of him. For Buddhism denounces all being, apart from form, as impossible. It is the purest Spinozism. It is identical with it. As all forms of true philosophy—whether Grecian, Egyptian, Eastern—all that rest upon a truth that, in this sense is truer than nature,—must rest upon Spinozism. We have said truer than nature ; for nature is not absolutely, but only relatively, true. It is only true in its forms, and its forms are not it.

But what a Spinozism are the doctrines of this Spinoza ! How apart from the vulgar notions of him and them ! How wronged, in the charges of utterest infidelity against him, has been the " God-intoxicated" man ! That arch-atheist, Benedict Spinoza.

They are quite right who come forward to resist this false view—or, rather, this no view—of Buddhism. That—and those truths which underlie the fabric of doctrines by means of which the religion of Buddha alone became possible to be apprehended by the intellect—is the sublimest inspiration. It needs not to penetrate very far into metaphysics to discover—or to suspect—the deep meanings lying hid under the first assumptions of Buddhism. Critics who have usually touched the subject have proved themselves commentators of forms only. They have, in most instances, failed utterly to touch the root of the matter. It is to be doubted whether they gather, in any way, the real force and meaning of the Buddhist philosophy.

Accepted with the literal eye, the tenets of the Indian theology, in reference to its Buddhist groundwork, appear to present about the usual average of mythologic fabling. But we judge upon the means of expression, not the thing expressed. That, in the very terms of expression, has escaped. As the reconcilement of that which " knows no sense," with apprehension through the means of sense alone, must always be impossible. Man's very being—that is, the laws by which he is, or his mind, shut him up, as it were, within themselves (or itself), as in a prison. And all his knowledge of things comes from that light shining *within* his prison—his mind. Within that radius, the light is perfect and he is himself perfect. But what guesses he, or can he know, of the great light without? That light, to him, may be no light. Light is material. Being, itself, only necessary to matter, and the life of it, or the soul of the world.

So taught the Persian believers in the one universal groundwork of light—the soul, or ultimate principle of everything to be known—which is the religion of the Magi, of Zoroaster, of the Guebres, of the modern Indian Parsees as of the middle-age European Bohemians; the remains of whose Fire-Palaces, or Fire-Temples, are yet to be seen, crumbling, indeed, into their own god, Light, around the reverend and time-battered, as well as war-battered, Prague.

Man is the centre to himself in his light of mind, shining as in his castle and prison of body. The forceful outer day—the god of the universal circle of things—once, in its violent inquest, fixed of a cranny and penetrating, would annihilate the temporary possessor of the tenement, and absorb all within (that is, him),ᶘto itself—laws to light; organism to broad being. Until reincorporate; that is, concrete.

Now, freed from technicalities, we will humbly

endeavour to give a view of the Buddhist philosophy.
And let who will, afterwards, say that atheism (in
the gross sense) cleaveth to it! That atheism which
means a denial of the personal, the tangible—the
real, if the accusers of Buddhism will have it so—
may go, indeed, with it. For that species of atheism,
that denial of a body, which body cannot be, which is
a contradiction in the very terms of thinking—rightly
seen, rightly taken, is but the exaltation of DEITY in
the philosopher's idea.

CHAPTER V.

IMMATERIAL PHILOSOPHY OF TIME AND SPACE.

THE Buddhist regarded all existence as evil, and the passage from state to state as the sort of self-shudder, or penance, or purgatory of nature; working itself free and disencumbering itself of matter, and of all its inconceivable, stupendous, and innumerable fashions and forms, and shades, and guises, upwards and outwards towards the universal light, the formless, emotionless, sense and life-exhausted supernatural and eternal REST. This it is which has puzzled all examiners of the Buddhist theory, in what manner to take, and towards a spelling at which we have seen some signal failures.

As Pythagoras believed, as Plato felt, as the mystics considered, as Berkeley and those who preceded him in the " non-material theory"—Hobbes and several other penetrating spirits—as these showed from various points of view, the ancient Indian sophists preceded all in declaring the hollowness of the whole of being. They declared life itself to be a show and an accident; consciousness they affirmed as a species of acknowledgment of imperfection; knowing a sort of radiation of power, which power, to be perfect, should have no movement, know no impulse, be incapable of finding itself. For aught can be found, identity can be established only by secondary means.

That which is self-existent need have nothing in which to exist. Otherwise the first shall be produced of the second, and be inferior to the second in the second being the glass in which the first knows itself. If "one" can be said to need "two" to discover itself as "one," the second, or the "two," shall be worthier than the first, or the "one." "Being," or "identity," shall be superior to that which underlies and makes it. In other words, the "machine" shall be superior to the "power," and the "forms" and "terms of life" shall be the "life" instead of the life. Or to put it more strongly, the creature shall be superior to the creator.

In the theory of the Buddhist philosophers, life being an accident, *something* has passed on and is passing on, behind to make it so. And this unknown, moveless, passionless REST, in which life should be impossible, being *form* or the Pythagorean number, is their *Nirvana*, or non-existence. Being their much-belied abyss of atheism; without God, since God is inconceivable except under being, and being, itself, is proved to be an accident. All power—that is, *all power put out*, being impossible to be God:—therefore God is impossible. But the mistake that is made, in the objections to Buddhism, is just this, that the objectors will insist upon starting upon the premiss that life is real. Ideas, by which we converse with that outside, are all which we are. And these are not real things, but mere delusive lights of the master phantom-light of intelligence. Hence divers ideas, as strength, power, education, circumstances vary. These being in the mind as the different colours and phases of the landscape, derivable from the light of heaven and the state of our optics. But is there any similitude of houses, trees, clouds, or any of these real outstanding independent objects, of a substance apart from the mere coloured mind, which, in its experience only, supplies it all? Take the human mind from the world and it exists no longer. The human mind *is* the world. It makes it. The world is as the show of optic glasses in the brain conceiving it, and outside of the living and active brain, no world either exists or can be conceived as existing. It is nothing. It can be nothing.

Philosophers have settled that space is nothing. It is nothing but that necessary to contain form—nothing but that necessary, for form, as the visible world, or man—or anything to be. It is merely created by that with which we measure, and is that measure. If we conceive space *per se*, we should cease to be, inasmuch as we should annihilate that law "which we alone are." Space is nothing, for we know it only by that which is in it. And to believe a thing which we cannot conceive is impossible. Nay, that thing cannot exist, else *any madness* may exist.

Time is nothing. It is simply a question begged, and a delusion settled, to make things exist. That is, it is necessary for man and the "visible" to be possible. Space and time are simply power : the very existence of which is a confession of limit and proof of want of power. As identity, or the necessity of identity, cannot be DEITY, else deity is secondary in the necessity of being. It negatives itself in knowing itself. Or, it is all and cannot be or know anything of itself further, and therefore it cannot exist. Cause and effect, Hume, and others long before him, settled—though the bond which holds all the "world" together—have no necessary connection. They are only the law by which things conceived can be. But if things conceived are unreal, the terms upon which they are, are alone a question begged. Therefore, if cause and effect have no vital and inseparable connection, and are only as the ground upon which this machine, the world, acts, and which ground has no existence out of the necessity of it, and out of the conception of it; and if the shows upon it are only things taken for granted—signs or symbols (as words of a language), meaning nothing for themselves but only having that meaning; in fact their existence, given to them, then miracles are—and must be in the nature of things—possible. Being only glimpses and interpretations and crosses from "other worlds," of whose laws we know nothing, and being as slips and rents in "this world," through which those other worlds rush occasionally in. Life is frequently *shaken apart*, as it were.

The lights—and shows upon those lights—of this world (as we all, at some times, feel and know), flicker like a *phantasmagoria*. The impression is really upon us at rare times—in our abstractions, in our deep thought, in our intense state of possession with an object, in the passing away of the spirit momentarily from out its chains of laws;—we feel at these times—*all feel*—the "ground" of mind—that is, our knowledge of the outside—as shaking faintly away from under our feet. We would appeal to self-consciousness, at those strong moments of our history of mind when the outer worlds and their intelligences pass in, or down, or up to us, for the more than suggestion—for the *persuasion*—that this, and we images upon it, which we know as the world, is as unreal as the cloud-kingdoms of mere thickened and enkindled space. This is the metaphysic Buddhist view.

All life is as a dust, through which the mysterious electric currents (the soul of the world, or final conceivable mechanical intelligence), pass and irritate. Move into those zones and patches of organisms rising and falling, gathering power and light and newer and grander forms, or sinking or rejected as farther and farther from that outward and upward glory—the mysterious and inexpressible transmigration of Pythagoras:—become Buddhist from the immortal and directly inspired teaching of the ancient, beyond expression, Indian philosophers. They, in fact, taught it first.

There is no solidity. All matter can be infinitely divided. There is no firm base to be reached. Man has not even matter in his hand. His instruments break before the exhaustless departments of nature. Even his boasted " solidity," of which he is so proud, gives him the go-by at every farther application of his wheels and screws ?* His moderate heat, child's-play at intensity,—stopped at even the enormous scale of 32,277 degrees of Fahrenheit, by Wedgewood's heat-measurer—is, notwithstanding all this, only a

* Each degree of Mr. Wedgewood's thermometer answers to 130 degrees of Fahrenheit; and he begins his scale from red-heat, fully visible in day-light.

bargain with nature that she shall not rush in, *with her own heat*, and consume him utterly and his whole toy-world. His domain of heat is a tame district, worn out—or granted—out of the whole floods of a supernal fire. This is ardency alone for spirits. Form was not made for it.

Why, thou wretched disbeliever!—Atheist—if that term of the beasts shall be pleasing to thee and gratify thy intense and yet thy meanest pride!—the circuits of the round world must be stored, thick beyond count, with the shapes, or shows, or souls of that escaped life—evolved out of its organisms—which from the beginning of time, whose comprehension shall pass almost from out the aching grasp of even the highest archangels—age upon age, cycle upon cycle—time, to whose evergoing clock the centuries shall count but as the seconds;—have almost worn its fretting rotundity *down* in the ceaseless, ever-growing, ever-bursting life! What if thou—with thy miserable optics—cannot see these realms of escaped vitality? Thy petty *radius* of sense shall not spread and circum-volve to these—devil-hampered and soul-muddied as thou art!—child of, and literal longer for the clods—dense, and dark, and thick as thine own soul—passed to the dust—since thou desirest it—by the Angels of God! Thy contemptible quadrant of senses shall not wheel to this glorious circle—struck to brilliance and God-lighted from within—of unimaginable know-ledge!—unimaginable by thee. Whose head is bent to the dirt, and whose thought-lamp, in thy dense darkness, is but as a glow-worm.

The whole round world is as a microcosm, whose

wonders are exhaustless; whose beauties are beyond expression; whose changes, whose decay, whose re-commitment into new forms is as the ceaseless revolve-ment of the Inexpressible Glory. Through the sea-floors and their multitudinous mimic continents, fruitful of moving life, fecund with their tree-growths and their semi-sylvan, semi-oceanic vegetation; through the clouds of the seas that rest or roll over them, through which speed the winged ships as golden (sunlighted) specks; through the hollow-crusted earth and its ridged rocks—earth torn and battered like a battle-beaten man of Eternal War, as it circles its resounding way amidst the roads of the lighted stars, "baring" to the changing Sun, and to the cold, renewing moon, its ploughed side, globing up, still defiant, with the wounds of the contentions of the centuries and with the retardation of the space-forces;—through the "built-work" of Nature, in short, runs the ever-coursing Inner Spirit, which forces, in its stupendous track (comet-like) the bordering matter into flame—to life!

Are not the sands kingdom-spaces for the infini-tesimally small life? Become not our microscopes as our telescopes, spying into the fields of space, and descrying therein the agitation of new worlds? Colours, forms, affections, sense-shapes fill the illimit-able depths of Nature, and pass from the " Lighted Nothing," through the panorama of figures, again into the "Lighted Nothing."

Is not all the world a woven tissue—wizard-coloured—of which the creative sun strikes the spangles into sparkling; stains, prismatically, with

the rose-hues of being, or the blues of decay—or,
rather, change?   Have not the old seas their forests,
and the prolonged sea-boards their blooms?   Roars
not old ocean with his caves; as the Nereid music
swelleth or sinketh, to fascination, loudly or faintly
through its shells?   Fires, and smokes, and springs, and
steam attest the attenuate bulk, spun through the hands
of the Great Magnetic Life, or by the power of the
Earth-God, into tissues.   What are the waves of the sea
but as the clouds to the sea-foundations?   What is as
the core, and the mighty heart of the great world, but
the spouting Fire?   Why be there not other lives in
that destroyer of *our* life?   What are the magnificent
air-shapes of our atmosphere; what the crossed cloud-
platforms of our sky; what the reduplicate and multi-
plicate fog-work and flocculence of the Western or the
Eastern Heavens, when the golden or the burning light
is poured through the heaped wonder-worlds of the
Magician of the Great Air;—what should be all the
cloud-settlings of our sky, but as the precipitate, and
dress, of the mere " used-up matter;"—glorious to our
senses, as even all the *refuse* is?   And if fire be, in its
own nature—so to speak—but the roaring-back,
illuminate, of Nature from the real unto the unreal
(as which the Magi teach, and as which the worshippers of the Element of Fire believe), then the very
excess of material light shall be but as the very *excess*
of the dense matter, remonstrating (as it were), itself
the brighter as it is, in itself, the blacker.   Nor are
these the vagaries of Philosophers, but world-old persuasions, when the vanity of knowledge had not made
a base " machine of wheels" of the world!

And if all this eluding matter escapes at either end as our nice knowledge fails, who shall say that, accompanying it, and a copy, spiritual, of it, and a worldless life out of the fact of it, and taking it up as man's sight and feeling of it render it up baffled (denying it, farther, however)—who shall say—we triumphantly repeat—that there are not "*lives on*" unextended to our experience, unknown and not to be understood of us, of nature different to all our perceptions of nature—the "many mansions" of which Christ spake—chains of being, and ways, and tracks, and means, and methods of existence, of which even the angels shall not know. Treasures of possible life—infinite regeneration and progressive perfection which lie, alone, within the capacity of—to our wretched human reason—that impossible thing, but yet, of all truths the truest—Omnipotence!

And let us rest with this sublime assurance. That the Kingdom of God lieth much nearer to us than consists in our vain imagination of possibilities. Yea, is at our door! God on our threshold! We all the while—Peter-like—denying him. Denying the Spirits because we cannot feel the Spirit!

The foregoing is the magnificent view of the Buddhists of Creation. Can we therefore wonder at the hold it has on its votaries?

CHAPTER VI.

BUDDHISTIC PHILOSOPHY OF LIFE.

MATTER, in the sublime Buddhist view, is as the disease, efflux, refuse, or necessary means, method or glass, for the one unknown Rest, or nothingness, to be possible. Power is suicidal. Denies itself. Is not, nor can be, God. And power—which is alone God—implies the necessity of that power. Which necessity is superior to that power; which, in this view, and it is all that reason can give us, is alone God. God—like every other miracle—is possible only in intuition. Reason falls to pieces in our hands in our attempts to educe God out of it. For God is all. As well call the stroke the giver of the stroke, as God-manifested, God-Real. This is the Buddhist view, which demonstrated manifestation impossible : and therefore effaced power, movement, a God out of the universe :— meaning all things that can be, or the HUMAN REASON. But this is simply annihilating all REASON, or matter, and making SPIRIT the one universal only life—God of another kind. In Everything and the Only. Surely, a doctrine most sublime, and—as the last and ultimate—inspired.

Exertion presupposes the necessity for the exertion. Which is insufficiency. Movement is doubt. "One" and "two" are impossible. For the second is the conviction and consumer of the first. It is superior to it, and is the "first" worked out to itself, demonstrated or completed, else it could not be. It over-rides and absorbs it, and is all it, in simply being:— proving the insufficiency of the "one." Power is disturbance;—which cannot be good. Out of the Nameless, from which comes Power, a third something is generated which is neither the first nor the second, but a sign; something accepted and different to either. But its "being" is its own "condemnation." And "being," or the "very possibility of being," is false in itself; though "necessary" for things to be possible. The first acts. The second is acted upon. And the third is the thing acted. The first is God. The second, in moving at all, contradicts the first as God, and effaces it. And the third is the Universe. Which alone remains. And this is untrue, and only a state, or condition, or mode, or bargain, or supposition, without any independent existence. Its laws are itself.

Now this is the Indian Trinity, as understood by the old Brahmin philosophers. And it is as equally Christian. For it lies deep buried in the foundations of metaphysics.

We underrate the great minds of antiquity in supposing that all of which man can think ; all that to which nature is capable of replying, was not thought out, was not obtained in the far-past ages. Religious are not new. Belief is not new. God is not new.

When we look out upon the world, and survey— whether as developed in ourselves or apparent else-where—this extraordinary thing called BEING, the first idea that we obtain of it is, that the very thinking of it is contradictory and negative. That, in fact, the

exertion of the mind is a thing against the purpose
and design of the world. That we were born to be
the " ideas," and not the " things thinking the ideas."
That the phantom-world of shows was, in reality, THE
world, and not the medium (or means) in which they
were exhibited. This very fact, if believed—which it
is never intended that it should be—would annihilate
body, and make the visions of things, or picture-like
ideas, the very things themselves. And not the *things*.

We have no business to think of thinking. We
are the thing itself (in the short word) about which
we strive to think. And the very first attempt to
stretch attention into conception is force, and therefore unpleasant; is—and there can be no doubt about
it—an effort in regard of the mental strength, greatly
resembling the unnecessary strength of the arm (abstractedly speaking) put forth in the bending of a
bow. That in our full health—*that in our perfect being
—that in our man's completeness*, we are the mirror,
or glass, of that outside (in its totality broken up, in
the very necessity of the thing, into parts or particles,
in order that, by succession or instalment, it may be
received), is a foundation-truth, to which, however,
we only become alive when we temporarily eject ourselves *out of ourselves* to see it. It is only in the
infinitesimally small succession of ideas, or the admission of them, and in the passing through of them,
one at a time, through this viaduct, or passage, or
narrow channel, or *means* of the constructive human
mind (that presses self, as it were, and makes ideas),
that the great mass or bulk of the " exterior" intensifies
inwards and concentrates itself, so to speak, into con-

ceptive atoms. To pass through, and to become aware of (in a sort of deglutition), in the "intelligence." Ideas pass through the mind like sand-grains filtrating through the fine long hollow of a shell, or as the exquisite atoms of the invisibly minute air through a tube, and causing the whistling, admitting (however instantaneous the succession) one grain or atom alone—as one idea alone—at a time.

Compound ideas, admitted as compound ideas, are impossible. And the very idea escapes in our attempt to make it an idea. So reluctant and so evasive are notions, and so singular a machine is the human mind, that the effort to form an idea (of ourselves, and by our own motion towards it, and not as the mere accepting it or admission of it as presented from the outside) is painful. And the very act is accompanied by a contraction, or is produced as by a sort of convulsion. A man contracts his brows when he endeavours to recall anything far behind in the magazines of memory, or when he seems to direct his mind (from itself) upon any external matter not admitted as our impression of the panorama from without, in which he is altogether passive. And the thought of a thing is a mentally muscular operation, in which there is the same kind of action as bodily action. The purely natural state of a man, without his own exertion from himself, is entire unmotived unconsciousness. Permitting the outside to flow, as it were, through him; as if the arch of a bridge should become the stream as it flows through it, or as if the glass should be the images reflected in the glass.

Two things, unlike each other, cannot last. Two

things, in the metaphysic sense, cannot be. Because, if they were both produced at once, they must be independent of each other, and equal powers and antagonistic powers, else they could not be separate. If they are alike, they must blend. If they are separate, they must be repulsions. But it is impossible they can both be equal, and not form one. For there must be a ground of difference to make them " two," and that ground of difference must be on the one side or the other. On whichever side the ground of difference may be, that side must be the inferior, in the fact of there being difference, and not completeness, to itself. The very admission of difference implying inferiority to that which hath no difference. Power is perfect and whole. There cannot be two powers, for the second power is only the first power under another name. First is all, or it is nothing.

If we examine the materials of which the world, in the general sense, is composed, we find it made up of substance, and of something which governs and rules, and constitutes that substance, which is spirit. Spirit has no *substratum* by which to produce results to us men. It has no laws, no rules, no precedence, no " one going before the other," nothing to be known by, nothing to be appreciated by. It deals with abstract qualities. It has nothing which we can see or handle. It is only to be understood as something moving on, and making sensible, exterior things. Now, as a man is a machine, or compound of certain motive powers, or senses, produced out of the affections of the matter outside of him, there is necessitated to him a medium, groundwork, or floor or basis, on which his powers or gifts (in other words, on which he, himself,) shall have operation.

Mind and matter may be two worlds identical, or rather one and the same thing. Of the world of matter we have means of cognisance in our senses, which walk upon it, breathe it, see it, hear it—in short, are made up of it and make it. As things, in the sense, are agreeable or otherwise, do we seek them or otherwise. And we call them good, or not good, as they happen to agree, or to disagree, with the senses that approximate to them, or that are their objects, or that, in fact, are the senses.

But this, when admitted to the uttermost, will carry us no farther than to a certain coincidence, and a certain happiness, to the several senses. And we only obtain, not a truth of real good, or real evil, but only a relation to the life which we live, and which—out of us—we have no business to affirm, and to take for granted, as any farther life than *our* life. That is, relation.

All that can be got out of the world is the third thing called relation; the point of the triangle, being neither the left-hand corner, which is power; carried along the base line into the right-hand corner, which is that "empowered" or acted upon; and both acting and reacting, to and fro, along the lower level, and directed and swept up to result, or end, or identity of both—being that new third thing, and only true thing—relation: or the point.

Why deal we with *comparison*, when the life of the swine is the perfectest to the nature of that swine? When the fill of evil is the perfection of the evil.

When the life of the bad man is just that life which
he, with an aim to excellence—that is, with the
insisting of the perfect conforming of means to end, of
patient and agent, of the squaring and regulating with
the objects to be squared and regulated, of the working up of the sum set him (in his bad man's nature)
to be worked up—should live.

Sin, or time, being the thing to be done, or shown,
by his bad nature, or " clock-work," who shall blame a
man for producing the very thing " set ;" the only thing
unavoidable?   His nature being to make something
of his nature, shall we quarrel with him, or say he is
wrong, in producing this very result?   We may as
well blame the sword for cutting, when therein it dis-
charges itself of its very duty.   In short, we are here
contending for the very faithfulness of nature, who
does her own best true work in presenting THAT—
and not that other thing—which her own constitution,
in the very vitality and completeness of the thing,
necessitates.   We hold with the soundest philosophers,
that nothing is imported into nature other than that
which is to be found in it.   That, self-complete to its
circumference, nothing from the outside, is, or can be
(from the nature of being), introduced from without.
It knowing nothing, and having nothing, of that
outside.

It is as if a man, asked to supply a means of
measuring that which, in its own nature, is incapable
of measurement, should offer his measure.   It is as if
an absurd person solicited, by means of colours, to
produce a picture, should seek to paint, or make-out,
or constitute his picture with the sums of arithmetic.

There is nothing surer than that two things, with no basis of likeness, cannot be both real. Matter and spirit have nothing in common. Therefore they cannot be both true. One must be unreal, and a deceit. And as, in the investigation into matter, the solids are lost out of the appreciative hands, it follows that there is no matter, and that the universe of things is all spirit. And that, as in the world of being we are not "spirit," and anything conceived must be in "being" or under form of some kind, therefore that all form, or being, is a show only, and unreal. All the real, *in its very necessity of-being real*, being empty of comparison (which makes being), and exempt of form and everything conceivable, and therefore (most logically and conclusively) nothing. Now, the sin or excess of "nothing," and its very denial and annihilation, is form, and the guiltiness of the "nothing-beyond-supposable" must be the "something-yet-supposable." And, therefore, "existence," or the "sense to itself," must be evil. Thus, demolishing matter, we superadd something better upon it.

Perfection is a relative term, having no connection with that thing which a man, in his self-deceit, calls good. Given an end—whatever machinery works towards that end; whatever means bring that end about :—what play of process realises that result, those means must be good, that end perfect. For the very idea of good, metaphysically, is only arbitrary vapour. The very notion of good, better, best; or bad, or worse, or worst, is a mere measure of comparison, or a spreading-out like any spreading-out, or opening-out, of completeness, perfection, or of nothing, to *make being.* We will illustrate our meaning by our example. A ray of light is white, colourless, object-less; is nothing. No eye-like machinery is set to decompose it, to untwine it out of its "oneness," to make comparison, or reality, or being out of it. It is nothing, has no existence, inasmuch as it has no laws, whereupon to set its *radii* of differences (like points of compasses), and circumvolve a world from out the start of them. How shall we attain to being (in other words, to reality of it), or of qualities, out of this non-entity? This non-existence is made by, and is, and is nothing *farther* than "laws" beyond which it cannot be conceived, nor can be anything. By force upon the thing, which must be *all* of the thing, since the mind can take in nothing farther of it, there shall be display, opening-out, analysis, "second out of first," divergence, comparison. And existence! Schopenhauser's thesis is cheerful: he says: *the exist-ence of the world is sin,* and its essence *misery.* Then come "laws;" then come "things;" then come affections; then come attractions and repulsions; then come movement and passion: in short, to the appre-hension, then come colours, or differences, or *other than nothing.* And between these worlds of affec-tions of body (called colours or differences) lie man and all possibility. Nothing conceived, or conceiv-able, being other than it. Beyond these laws and necessities of being (in being) there lies nothing. It standing as the Eternal-Matterless, in which there lie no world of shows, in their vexatious undulations, and in their necessarily deceiving (for life to be) manners, to cause comparison. No realm of matter, in the ever-changing modifications of unity, or the "uniform," or the "nothing," through which (in the solid sense) to move the sensible, the ever-producing, and the ever-creating magnetism or Life.

The spiritual gulf of nothingness which (in the metaphysic, that is, in the humanly-reasonable, or false, idea) is, and can be, alone, God, it is impossible to conceive as mind or an underlying means, or, so to speak, as the floor of sensitive and lightening and cogent Power. Over which to go rolling the mind-forces in their ever-spreading, slackening, swelling or subsiding, individual, subsidiary and self-exerted appetence and strength. In short, outside of laws and necessary shows—exterior of the splendid, motived, coloured, and sun-sense illuminated rings of life, in which deceived, and necessarily deceived, man is struck the centre (as the wondrous spark to find them fellow-fire, and false), lies nothing—or matter-less. Passionless Rest. To which Rest the Buddhist assures that all form, or seeming, or illusion, or purgatorial "swathes," or confines of cogence and life, or "being," in its amplitude of meaning, is tending. Controlling and centrifugatory from off the great central and immortal Light, where motion and comparison, or good, or better, are unknown, but all is Rest and nothingness. This is the world of sense, or as in the waves of experience, or as in the procession of the cycles, or as in the fields, and wreaking into show, of TRANSMIGRATION, like the multiform and ever-brightening, ever-blackening, ever-self-thinning, and ever-purifying, smokes. Birthing and carrying over their own nature, in the restless wheel, as greater

E

or as lesser, as grander or as baser, as the holier or
the worse, through time immemorial—made only time
in the measure of the changes—each and centrically
seeking, in return, to that SPLENDOUR of NOTHINGNESS,
from which issued, first, as expiation, and, as existing,
forms (to, therefore, expiate, of body), all things knowable, and, therefore, all things bad—all "being," and,
therefore, all consciousness.

This is the great gulf of Nothingness, or of broad,
unmotived Spirit, or of immortal Fire, clear and vacant,
into which everything must he committed—everything
cast, of the conceivable, to be lost of itself. This—
as the great material element of Fire can swallow all
things, of the worlds, in its devouring jaws; scarching
through, and taking in, their essences, into itself—
rather insinuating itself through, and disclosing its own
glorious countenance, through their far-sundered atoms,
till the very solid matter shall disappear; fire opening,
from the centre, out as the broader floor, down to
which, in our chemic, penetrating exploration, searching through the media of evolution, we have at last
awfully come! all nature being rendered up in its
fierce search, and in its not-to-be-contradicted (in the
world) forces and truly supernatural power.

Possibility collapses in the very idea of an addition
to unity. Since that which cannot exist of itself, and
needs something else to make itself real, must have
only a leaning, begged, and permitted nature—altogether false and contradictory. Divinity must be
complete and clear (out of idea), and therefore nothing.
Or, in being, it is at once as the "glass," and not the
"thing showing in the glass," and as divinity is only

possible under idea of it, which is not the thing but the *idea* of the thing, and as the idea of the thing is the only thing possible (if we are not ourselves God), there is nothing other than the show, and no divinity at all. The world being it or God, or the human reason. Thus the human *reason* infallibly, under all its various heavenly deceits and just the more successfully according to its perfection, leads FROM God, and the idea of God (which is not God) is the very opposite of God, and being the very opposite of God, it must be the Evil-Principle. Nothingness is the non-holding of idea; of comparison, defect, or the devil—exempt and blank of meaning. Nothingness, as containing nothing; first "all," knowing no devil of "second" to find itself "first," and therefore (in the fact of being) conquered by the devil to discover itself, or be, at all. The reader will perceive that we are arguing for the Holy Spirit.

All this will only go to prove that, in the mere *human* reason, or *idea*, God is annihilated, and that he is only ultimately and really possible in the divine immediate possession, or in the supernatural *trampling* on Idea, and (to the world) madness or ecstacy. We can never rise to Him. He must descend to us. We can never make God. He must make us. He is only possible in thus snatching us out of the world, or out of ourselves. Michael-like, trampling us, and extinguishing us (Satan-like) first utterly out of idea. Which is the world, in which if we search for Him we shall fail to find. Otherwise, in miracle. Which miracles are disbelieved of the world, to be the very truest, and, in its disbelief, to be *made* true. That only true, being that not apparent. The faces of martyrs and saints, and the visible glory shining in them, as being not of the world, are the best proof— even to flesh—of God! Nothing of this miracle can be, else, got out of the things of the world. Nothing more distinct than in the transfiguration of the Holy, that, in miracle, have been illuminated out of flesh. And this is the cause, and the reason, of sainthood, and the why of its worship. It being substantially, and in verity, God.

And the disbelief and denial of Sainthood is the proof not only that it is true, but that the world— including human reason—is of evil, and is the devil; and, in denying it, the very thing not true—that being the only truth, and the other show only, to " cause existence," which is true only in the belief of it. That is, as man is.

As the subtle spirit of the under-lying, and behind all nature, ambushed Fire, can throw all the chains of the great world loose, and spin the solid matter (in its waving wheels of the furnace), until it evaporates and delivers it up, expanded free, out of the touch of sense, so as at last not even unweighable gases, or clouds, or colours, into the great void; so, into this great, all-swallowing, fiercely unappeasable, utterly bottomless abyss of the resolving, melting, sundering, and evapo-rating splendour of metaphysic or Buddhist nothing-ness, can be cast all mind and all the delicate piecework of mind, all the qualities, all the affections, all the good, all the bad, all law, all form. In short, "all better and best," and the very power of thinking, as all the utterest consistency, or thought, worlds, or reason, or anything.

CHAPTER VII.

THE THEORY OF CASTE.

LYING deep in nature are the differences between man and man, race and race, tribe and tribe. Physiology teaches us that all animal life—indeed all life—is alike in one respect, that of an extraordinary and even excessive chainlike succession. It is at the breaks, twists, and turns or knots; or at the over-passing and at the singular leaps, as it were, in the one grand system of organisms, that we catch nature the most successfully, and *detect* her, so to speak. For she is, herself, deceitful, seen with the philosophic eye; sly, imposing upon man with her shows and making him in them. For, melting out of her shows, she ceases.

The position of the equality of man is a fallacy. Neither souls nor bodies are equal. As bodies are superior or inferior as the place in the scale is determined as higher or lower, as flesh and blood are scarcely flesh and blood in some instances, as the human assimilates to the brute, referred downwards, or rises to the angelic, extolled upwards—the magnetic influences through which all are produced, perhaps swelling or sinking under the impulse of the penetrating, outside, supernal force, supervital power, or "gods," under whatever name, the agents of the "All"—so the very coarseness of the manufacture betrays the origin. The stamps are stamped for inexpressible periods, subject only to reclamation through the divine mysterious Lifting, using circumstances as the outward stuff or dead matter out of which to work.

Man is much nearer to the lower animals than, in his absurd self-possession or pride, he imagines. He has flattered himself too much. His wants, his method of production into this world—and his beyond expression mean departure from out it (or so natural falling into the earth again as dust), is his stigma— —is the proof to him that he is absolutely of the family of those which perish—that he is hope-lessly of that which is matter. He is dense, soulless, worthless refuse, except in the Divine Immediate Possession or Seizing.

Certain grades of men being of this low class— certain sections of creature partaking so much of the brute—certain races possessing so very low and dim a supernal illumination that the light shall flicker down into ashes; into the mere brute-instinct of machinery—tribes of people, even of the one nation, being so created—or recreated—made or formed of base usages, of low aliment, of a hopeless bondage of everduring investitures of circumstances; and this not for a life only, but inherited and passing, in the infinite succession of generations, into new nature, or sustaining, without progress, in the one nature— lying, at the outset, at the base of the scale, and never, perhaps, in man's limited memory to be lifted —for man's memory is short; these classes of people present, we urge, the aspect of totally distinct and different *strata* of life; band below band, refusing to incorporate (as fire and snow start from each other, and, in forbidden embrace, mutually kill); never mixing—never to mix—never possible to mix, except in some violation of the primordial universal law of no retrogression—no backward turning, but all advance and spreading out, radiating from the one central Immortal Point—the centre-pin upon which the whole magnificent scheme of God's universe is turning, throwing off and evaporating its coarser fires, urging from the middle-most inexpressible Light, which in its urgence, in its pulsations, in its efforts to find itself, creates, and magnifies into forms, and disengages off itself, and parades even as writhings are paraded as grand things in their very agonies, those wondrous varying shows of life which the founders of Buddhism—eighteen hundred years before the Christian religion—named *Maya* in its various degrees, or the universal Kingdom of Necessary Delusions.

This is the origin of *castes*, in the Hindoo's view of nature. He acknowledges not the equality of man. He teaches not that the same soul is alike to be found in all mankind. He takes not her weapons, or means of working and method of being, out of nature's hand. He elevates not man when she says *this* is the narrow circle in which this or that class of being shall traverse.

And they shall change their nature, doth she add, and win down more of the light which is as the " floor of light" to the Kingdoms of cloud-flux, which are raised the thicker over it that the creatures may be the thicker—smoke, for a medium, that sense-things may be in it. Otherwise, shall creatures become raised—before, in repeated and perhaps multiplied transmigrations in other fields of *Maya*, or illusion, than in this life, they become purified, and are, perchance, out of God's laboratory, and in God's good time, reproduced as other souls, elsewhere, in another and a nobler grade. Remission back in another life, or when again reproduced on this planet, is the Hindoo view of failure of good life, or of the non-urging up and outwards imposed, as the Divine Law, on the lives here.

The Brahmin denies that low caste, and high caste, are any more the same, than that the poplar is of the same family with the larch; the humble, unregenerate moss, or the prickly, vicious, roughly-grained thistle, of the same rank as the tall, straight-growing and free-growing grass, singing in the summer, in its pride, and waved in the glorious breeze, any more than that the ferret or the polecat, the foul rat and the gross-feeding pig, whose obscene sty is in every wealth of garbage—these, as the very Pariahs and outcasts of the four-footed races, base in their very bad blood and rough-making, through the witch-like and Satanic cross-forced and foul-forced assimilation, are of kindred destiny, and of equal cleanly and happy composition, with the swift and silken antelope, or the noble-stepping Imperial Lioness.

Creatures are of that they eat. Aliment becomes body; becomes as much soul as that circumstantial and eliminated soul can admit. We are of our food, elaborated by the secret magnetic laws of nature; which, out of food, precipitates body, and, out of body, extols mind—or all that we can know as mind. The higher animals, in instinctive self-maintenance, scorn and abominate the offal which is the appropriate and natural producer and soul-maker—so to speak—of the baser creatures. Which are degenerate even from "dead dirt," in being further accursed and convict " in life." Living and walking corruption, affirmative and risen up, defiant, against the eternal matterless:—the One Rest; unformed; knowing neither Space, nor Time, nor Being.

The Hindoo follows, in fact, that which he finds in nature. Deep-buried in it, he found eternal divisions in men. He leaves their conversion—the use of the materials—in God's own hand.

And out of black he will not seek to educe white. He shall not make the elegant stag mate with the grosser sloth. The winged inhabitants of the mid-day light heavens, flushed to dazzling in the glory of the tropics, he shall not rate with the yellow-footed kite, or confound with the ink-black rook or the carrion vulture. He shall not even mingle, in idea, the silver fish with the grubs. The glittering companies which have the clear-flowing waters for their spread celestial palace, he shall not associate with the grosser creature-growth springing and multiplying from the mosses and the teeming water-ferns, and yet as knots of life unlocomotive. He shall not enforce or do the indignity to nature to make consort with the fairy-fish, the slimy eel—cursed for his glutted creeping, like the earliest. Snake devil-circling under the retributive heel of the convicting Angel! He shall not esteem the lifeless creepers, or the tribes of worms or green-glowing insects, or the hirsute, or monstrous, or glutting children of the quickened desert, starting to animal alarms, or of the poisoned marsh whose clouds are gnats—he shall not confound this obscene efflux with the awe-exciting, the perfect individuality of the princely panther, or the haughty terrors of the great eagle—Imperial among Birds.

For the creatures are of their feeding. Their soul is of the blood and flesh which make it. They are, through and through, of their bodies, in fact; and are as a part suffused into nature, so to speak. Clean or unclean are they as nature—so to put it—shall have no arrest, no clog, no return—again back upon itself. Which contrary-working produces corruption, and which is the devil-marked violation of the Immortal Law, the harmonious, uninterrupted radiation, or upward and outward spreading; glory seeking, perfection seeking.

Man dies every day in his own native bodily corruptions. But his living, healthy existence is a witness to God. He is, in his clear health of mind and body, as a precious vessel in which God's light shall shine! Or he shall be literally as a foul tomb in which matter flocks, and thickens, and blackens, and *lights again!* until its very devil-like animation and its horror-light— of dead matter no longer—shall be its own conviction and curse—aye, its own self-consuming curse! Such is life, and the purity of life; and the opposite of the purity of life.

Out of the gross-feeding creatures whose soul is their food—"*and which shall he eat?*"—the Hindoo essays not the vain task of eliminating the rainbow colours. These shining up to the eye, and produced in light in that thousandfold sifted matter, spun to utter purity, known as air. The last of himself that is to man, short of the lucent spirit-medium in which the senses— in which he, himself—dieth. As a creature that cannot live in it. And this is the Hindoo philosopher's doctrine of his castes.

Who shall say that it is a doctrine false or wrong, and not a belief the surest and highest? Requiring, however, philosophy to understand it. Requiring patience to master it.

Believing, as the Brahmin does, that he is removed by, perhaps, countless generations from clearance out of matter, of which, even in infinitely finer *media* than those to be grasped of sense (in the human acceptation of sense), his first series of heavens or removal to a higher though still corporeal or embodied state is to consist; believing that, like the waves of the seas of illusion (*Maya*, or *Maia*, in its thousandfold progressive sensitive cinctures, undulating on to its final self-disengagement of deceit, evil, matter, or being at all, as far as he can understand it); illusion in which he alone is, and in which, too, he is the meanest appreciable point: concluding that to advance in the scale of being that which is eliminated into, that becomes and makes his soul, namely that which is incorporate into and makes and fabricates that machine of sense which he knows himself, including that sensitive aggregate or sum, spread out before and after, in *media*, which he calls his soul or power of thinking, or rather, *capacity of soul-seeing*—concluding that this fine edge or mirror of life must not be debased into living corruption, or lost in soul-fogs (or damnation, or reference back into the *darkness of matter* in the Pythagorean sense), as which certain foul tribes of creatures which have souls, or sums of senses as foul, in their natures are and must of necessity be; the Brahmin refuses to embrute, or destroy, or compromise the IMMORTAL POSSIBILITY within him by absorbing into himself, adopting, incorporating, or chemically identifying into his own body (and therefore into all that he has of soul), base, corrupt, and damned souls—already the things of perdition. In other words, it would be as throwing open the doors of his own being that the devil might enter! Could he do this—believing this—and not blaspheme?

He would thus be, himself, breaking the law of universal advance ; eating, as it were, his own spiritual ruin. Circle after circle, in endless yet multiplying rings, extends out the circumference of created creatures. The universal, indescribable *medium*—the soul of all things that can be—lives through them. They are the flux of each stage. The evil, scum, or lees of life possess, and make, and are, and have subsided into the lower creatures.

The Hindoo must not make his soul that which is lower than his soul. He breaks the Almighty Law of Progress to recede. So long as the waves of organisms flow out from the Grand Centre without check or devil-irritant return back in upon themselves, the law of the Deity is maintained. Such things are spiritually clean. All is harmony, or all is clean. But at certain points, deep-buried in the flows of time, the Oriental thinks he can discern particular knots, back-returns, and wreaking in upon itself (existence,

rebellion, devil-stirring); corruptions in the great
scheme of Being, in fact; coagulation, clots, can-
cerous points in nature, from contact with which
springs Spirit-Danger not to be told; from which a
super-death (for death here is life elsewhere), or the
Immortal Death, blasting with defect the whole design
of things, may be inherited. The unpronounceable
sin; the unforgiveable sin.

These are as devil-spots in the fair flesh of a God-
made nature (necessary, otherwise the world would
not be a place of progress, but a heaven); these are
innately corrupt places to which the baser elements
instinctively rush, and where they break (so to speak)
as the confession of the defect, the rottenness of the
whole: that so finely spun, attenuate and sense-
coloured universal Globe of Being. To be one day
trodden into dust—aye, the whole Universal Being—
like the bubble which it is, beneath the triumphant,
the reclaiming foot of the Almighty Master, the
Maker!

Of these foul living things—swine stand as the
highest (or sink as the lowest); that execrated, cross-
growing, living form, into which, as the basest that
this whole world of shows could show, the Saviour
permitted the dispossessed devils to seek refuge. This
from his god-like rebuke! Goats, reptiles, all creeping things and the whole tribes of shellfish, or *exuviæ*,
are also foul to the Eastern.

And the Hindoo theologians proceed upon this
assumption. Life upon life (for they make this term
of "vermin" much more comprehensive than we do,
as their sensual ethics are infinitely more delicate)

they hold in utter horror. Oysters, creatures in shells,
spawn of all kinds, they deem the seething, corrupting-
back again into life upon the very edge, border,
fat or excretion of life. All these living things—all
that, from this highest point of view, shall show as the
unnatural and fecund *vexation into life anew*, as it
were; all this devil-life or rot-life (to put the case in
its strongest but its truest light), bred out of the very
fierce contradiction, irregularity, back-coming, vice,
matterful or devil-like impetus, or that hypergene-
rating, or in and in rotten-procreativeness which is
the very excess and sin (God permitted, for life to be)
of the immortal luxuriance and indispensable overpower of the creation—working in its thousand
prodigious ways.

Darkness and Light are brother and sister. We
should know no light without darkness. For darkness
is but the irritation of the darkness into light to see
itself. Light is begotten (the brighter from the
blacker) of darkness simply. Light is darkness, indeed,
wrought visible, and is the soul of matter; the fiercer
the deeper we go out of our sensations. Thus Light,
itself, is no less material than all other visible things.

"Shall I defile myself in eating Death?" asks the
Hindoo. "I am not eating flesh," he urges, "when I
partake of the unclean thing. I am accepting into
my being—for I am my body, apart from God in me,
which may or may not seize—that which shall banish
me from the eternal light, that shall condemn me to
ages of penance in, but momently in centuries perhaps,
approach lightwards, perfectionwards from the hell of
beasts! Shall my pure blood, shall my clean flesh,

shall my clean soul, which is the sum and lightness of both; shall this pellucid commixture be muddied, be poisoned with the corrupt elements of the creeper? Shall these matter-fogs clog my light? Shall my soaring spirit, God-beckoned, drag its soiled and devil-clutched wings backward until eternally befouled in the venomous mind of perchance the unutterable and hopeless supernatural corruption? Shall I mate myself in fleshly and loathed bonds, shall I yield into the souls of the condemned and densest brutes, receptacles of the accursed? The forms, so to speak, into which nature empties its devil-offscourings.

"For I believe in the immortal things—the sure things which underlie, and fashion, and use as a workman uses his material, and which make—far out of this nature—the meaningless shows of a *world which is only true in our man's acceptance of it.* And which shows alone are the curse. As the feet of clay to the head of gold—sun-emblazoned—upon which feet of clay shall alone the divine image go!

"Defilement by touch—temporary debasement by contact—exterior personal mischief, I can efface, I can wash out in the sacred streams; the pure flows of the (save air) farthest separated, lightliest sifted matter. I can wash, and I can be again clean. But the forbidden thing once eaten, once assimilated, once become of my blood, mingling the devil-element, flooding that, as it were, by hyperphysical world of magnetic atoms—centres of attraction and repulsion —which, philosophically, I know I am, with the very thick soul, the nourishing and producing medium of the beasts—that very densest, devil-massed matter

(by the immortal law), from which I am trying to
escape. And my soul—which I thus make my body
—is ruined, as by own signing of this Fiend-instrument,
on and through the eternal roads of the inexpressible
future—the everduring, everpassing-on To Be. And
I groan—spiritually—deep down in the mountain
pile of life scenes (*Maia*); from extrication altogether
from which (as false and evil), even from the whole
Breadth of Life, as from its highest to its lowest,
stage upon stage, grade upon grade, world upon
world beyond calculation, do I supplicate, in prayers
and in agonies, the Divine Master. For escape from
this, and for the taking me unto himself, do I ceaselessly entreat, in his own unutterably wise time, the
Lord of the Absolute. He who has elected Life as
the medium, as the penance, as the purgatory,
through which the immortal soul—through which all
COMPARISON—shall purify back towards his Eternal
and Perfect Throne. Otherwise, out of illusion, into
rest from show, or into NOTHINGNESS! Into the
HEAVEN of NOTHINGNESS!"

And these beliefs, so altogether misunderstood and
vilified, not that the believers were so irrational, but
that their vituperators were incompetent; not that the
language was wrong, but that it was rejected as
a jargon by those only who (not knowing it) could not,
of course, understand it; these are the points of the
Hindoo creed which are so rashly and—in the philosophical sense—so *coarsely* denounced.

Do the denouncers limit the manifestations, and
the methods of teaching, of the Deity? Are the
great truths subject-matter for the settlement of

churches and chapels? Can these unphilosophical objectors render reasons for their assent to the fundamental points of their *own* Christian theology? Do they understand them? Are they thinkers sufficient? Are they rhapsodists adequate to grow alive to the holy mysteries?

Their common sense—so vaunted as all-equal—and their reason of the schools, break asunder, like all mathematics, like all measures, before abstractions, before the last truths. Methods and means fail when transported into a scene where the very mathematics —supposed the solidest among the things of the world—melt as into nothing! What shall become of measures and of measuring, there where both are *impossible*—where laws (any more than forms) exist not—where the parade of arithmetical figures that should teach to the reason, disappear in the intuition which teaches *all* without machinery to teach? Comprehend the great, evading, occult truths of your own creed; reconcile the (to common sense) contradictions of the religion which you, yourselves, avow —the beliefs by which you swear before the one Almighty God, whom, in his various dispensations— Christian or heathen—we *all* worship; before in your blindness, in your prejudiced, in your mad assumptions without enquiry, in your so absurd taking for granted that this or that shall be so because you choose to make it so out, and before in your unreasoning passion you raise this pitifully weak, this only spiteful outcry against things which you do not understand— which you *refuse* to understand!

" Know us, know our religion ;—nay, look into

F

your own religion," exclaims the Eastern—"before in
your convenient rage—in this your so suddenly-
awakened zeal rather for the God of Gold than for
the God of Poverty, of Suffering, and of Universal
Pity; before with your fierce denunciations of our-
time-out-of-mind ancient creeds—noise to hide con-
fusion—you yell against that for which *we*, after all,
are not to blame! But for which arraign Incalculable
Time.

"Charge our Teacher, the Immortal Time, with
these things. Make the mute Anarch answer! Full
of the centuries. Draw nearer to God, yourselves,
rather than invoke destruction on us!

"If you will, yourselves, have nothing of philosophy, stand alone upon that brute force which shall—
as it before hath done—make you material master
so long as there is body for your body-laws to wreak
themselves through. Ask, in your sane moments, of
yourselves—demand of your thinkers—of our religion,
which we uphold as the most delicate truth, as the
soundest and the ultimate ethics—that is, undeformed
with its base earth-adjuncts, grown up, under world-
rooted systems, in India, as time went on. What
are these but as the dross of the jewel, the gross
weeds cumbering the spotless marble as it rises a
palace-monument? Seek and ascertain if ours is
not the highest, and the holiest, and the grandest,
and the sublimest system of philosophy—this
Buddhism—which the world ever saw! Identical
in its basis even with the eternal foundations of
your own Christian belief on your own side—
purgation through suffering into glory. Question

—as is fit—with the urgency of a real matter of life and death, the unbiassed human intelligence, left free to itself to judge, and we anticipate your avowal. Yes, it shall indeed be that the old Indian revelation, the most ancient in the memory of man, is not alone the truth, but that it is the parent of your own—nay, of all the truth of all consistent and philosophic creeds—truth of truth!

"God is not the God of the fashions of world-beliefs, but of the possessed soul. He is not the God of Religions, but of the mute, light occupied and killed-to-this-frame-of-things adorer. The upward gazer, but not downward fashioner. The rapt soul raised to heaven, not the groper amidst the manners through which, and by which, to express the uneasy sense of the consciousness of the existence of a Heaven, and the desire to escape upwards to it!"

And it is surprising how strikingly the inexpressibly ancient religious laws of the Gentoos accord with the prohibitive regulations of the Mosaic inspired code. Lying deep in the universal truths of things must be the cause which instituted certain matters as sins; which declared a range of pollutions, from which the easy-living, irreligious moderns, profess themselves standing free.

But the question may well be asked. Are they indeed free, or only, in their degeneracy, and perhaps in their worse destiny, thinking themselves free? For the worlds are all before, and this mere unit of existence is of small comparative value. Are they indeed embruted, as it were, in their own ingenuity, and their mechanical "this world" laws?

Eating and drinking, back into their own husks of life, so to speak, and not living them off with God!

The following may seem an extraordinary position, but even modern philosophical researches into the phenomena of things, seem to demonstrate it as something not to be instantaneously rejected.

The old Buddhists—as equally as the ancient believers in the doctrine of the Universal Spiritual Fire—held that Spirit Light was the floor or basis of all created things. The material side or complement of this Spiritual Light being Fire, into which element all things could be rendered; and which (or Heat) was the motive of all things that are. They taught that matter or mind—as the superflux—as the sum of sensations, or as natural and unreal shows of their various kinds—were piled, as layer on layer or tissue on tissue, on this immutable and immortal floor or groundwork of Divine Flame, the Soul of the World. That emotion, intensity, mind-agitation, thought, according to the powers of the unit or the lifting heavenward:—or as the dots or dimples in the ever-flowing onwave of being: were—to speak in the familiar sense—"as impressions down," perhaps through and through its covers, upon this living floor of spiritual flame. The escape of which was the magnetism—magnetism of the body: supersensual force, or miracle, of the spirit—which is the disclosure of and bond of the Universe, and the "self-protest" of matter, remonstrating again back, as it were, towards its last HEAVEN or REST. Which latter is the "non-irritation into matter," or sublime "Non-Being" of the Buddhists.

CHAPTER VIII.

THE REVELATION OF LIGHT AS THE FUNDAMENTAL PRINCIPLE OF ALL MYTHOLOGIES.

THE revelation of light, in two species, natural and spiritual, and its conflict with the powers of darkness, is the fundamental principle of all the mythologies. It is the Indra, or Veeshnou, of the Hindoos, the Osiris of the Egyptians, the Zeus of the Greeks, the Odin of the Scandinavians, and the Yang, or perfect substance of the Chinese. As the fiery darkness, in like manner, is represented by the opposition of Ahrimanes, of Typhon, of Pluto, of Loki, and, in the Chinese system, by the principle Ya, designating imperfect matter. The analogy between the sun of this world and the rational light, on the one hand, and between materiality and mental darkness on the other, causes the connection between theology and cosmogony in all the ancient systems. And it is this perpetual comprehension of two ideas in one symbol that has given rise to so much perplexity in the interpretation of the old fables.

Of the solids composing this thing called world, and forming, as it were, the blocks, or stones, out of whose congruity, and arrangement, and disposal into beauty, into grandeur, and into sublimity, considered in the one and the agreeable view; and into discomposure, into alarm, and into horror, regarded in the other (the more natural perhaps; of the sounder

foundation and certainly the more immediate and
cogent, as fear comes out of body); and the more
painful and least happy:—of the matter or
bulk of this phenomenon (solid though it be)
of the world, there are varieties of which neither
can we see the first nor the last. Richness, variety,
abundance, prevail where the heated forces are most
livelily at work. Matter becomes harsh, stringent,
self-denying, economic (and, as it were, leaden), as
cold hath more to do with it. All the sentimentally
sensible or abstract qualities, too, subside as fervour
fails with them. The evolvement out of the lower
and lower bases, or floors, or leaves of life become
less special, less distinct. To borrow a phrase from
another sense, less "loud," as infinitely less affluent
or wealth-creating (growing out of its very increase),
as the heats diminish in dealing with them. Glory,
grandeur, beauty, power grow and intensify as
that hand upon nature, called *heat*, closes the firmer,
holds the more continuously and grapples the fiercer.
In the fierce heats of the heat-anvil come out the
glow and the colours of the great artificer's work of
the overpoweringly splendid creation. In the multi-
plyingly coloured flames of the tropical heat, glow-
out, and grow, (the intenser and intenser out of its
own restlessly eager *getting*,) all the grand special
things, all the brilliant utter-birth, all the glorious
worlds of colour out of colour, of agitated and
populous light, out of light, out of the several spread
rays. And of the solid things which evolve to be
spun into ideas of them through the loom of man's
apprehension, the trodden machinery to work of which

comes out of the *same things*, to him, as senses—making the man that outside—we find the solidest show of matter, called metals. In a ton of which may be a whole world (compressed) of that thing falsely called space, because, with our rough means of dipping, we cannot, as it were, lap the infinitesimally fine water out of it. Marbles, the stones of their various "broods," with their many-sparkling and coruscant tears, called jewels; the flints with their waving veins and laminated, glancing, and onyx-like nodes or nodules, and lime or marl clots; and the cleaving, hard-skinned minerals, with their struck fractures (which will not part save with the forceful clip, slicing their, so to speak, iron-grey, and gravel-like golden, and bistre-brown, and raw-red flushes) : —all the rocks and spires of the world, and the vein-work, tree-like net of metals, wandering, like nerves, or the rudimentary "nerve-matter," through the Telluric body, are the solidest, firmest display of that foundation-floor, called matter. The deeper in density that nothing material can be supposed deeper than them ; the proof of the bulk of them, or their fiercest atomical clinging-together, being that opposite of airiness and the sum of all world-powers, weight.

Now this word, weight, signifies that, of the world, you have enough of it. Since, if there were nothing of it, or of the clinging and holding-together, and grasping of matter, called gravity, the fine world of this clever sense-thing, called man, would *evolve*, so that there should be nothing of it, or of him, left. The whole tightly-wound chain flying off into that widely-starting circle that, to the destruction of mathematics, should settle not even into *arc*, but fling farthest into ever-hopeless straight line! The very mathematics come out of the contraction in idea, and are no more, and have no more reality than those ideas already—and long ago settled in the past philosophically thoughtful ages, when men were heirs into supernatural God-thought—found out to be nothing. This illustration will subsidiarily serve to show that, *out of mathematics*, man can have no ideas. And that, as mathematics are only found in the making of a world, and that, as they are impossible upwards and off from a centre, or a law which makes itself, neither mathematics, nor the world which they make, can be true. Any other than in the mere *show* of the making. No farther true, we mean, than the thing itself, or in the *downward* force into sense to "make the making." Out of the revolvement of the world, and the tight-drawing of the senses into conviction, spring-back—liberating from the force upon them—the contractive and constrictive thoughts into "straight line." And therefore—since line, even in the mathematical sense, is only continuity and not figure—into "non-being." We get not the *bend*, so to speak, to make a world.

The densest and thickest things are the metals and stones. These graduate in heaviness, and have more and more of weight as there is more and more, in them, of tight-clinging adhesion. Next come the earths and marls, the atoms of which are held farther and farther apart, and which have *that between* to keep them, as it were, at arm's length. These are the easier wrought, with lesser force, as there is the less exertion necessary to roll their masses of atoms, as it were, over and over. Then come the fibrous matters, which have growth coming out of them ; and which, out of themselves, evolve certain motived demonstrations, which we recognise as something other than dead, undesigning matter.

Growth is, indeed, a strange thing. What is it but the evolution of invisible, deeplying, and undiscoverable worlds, urging up from somewhere, through a point, as smoke will issue from a vent? And using this world (on the other side and to the things in it) as a medium of display, panoramic space, to be sketched over with figures. What is growth but a universe of passage on to another "elsewhere," which other "elsewhere" the growth takes and passes up into when we miss it out of this? Underneath, and before this, are floors of things which are only *not yet* as being not yet possible to our sense of them. We catch them in their passage, when they fall under the motive laws which make them to us, and make us in making *them*. We say that they are not when *we*, only, can know nothing of them. And we declare that they are extinct, when they have merely sunk, as under our horizon, or gone like our own experiences of the past years. Which yet are, though we have passed on and left them behind. As we pass through rooms, or leave objects, on either hand, as we go a journey under the morning, afternoon, or evening lights, which, each, has sentiments and glories of its own ; as well say of ships out of sight, that they are not because we see them not. Man's life is only his *entourage*. All else is as unsound as any other fable which he causes only to exist in his lying belief, and this is begotten only of the false thing upon itself.

Solid, unliving things increase only by aggregation. Nought is added out of other worlds (that is growth). All comes out of this. The mountain is only an aggregation of stony parts. The sea is only an increase of more and more water. But living things, whose means of elimination out of other worlds into this world is articulation, and, in the higher range of living matters, organs, or machinery, of getting from elsewhere—obtaining from other places than here in this given quantity of matter, called world—really win in their own self-generating :—being as the hinge on which both worlds turn. That world of the visible and that world of the invisible—in mutual complement and flowing into. What is water but the solid matter whose particles are so much farther and farther started asunder, and yet not struck so wide as to have the affinity sundered? In waves, the fine matter rolls over in mechanical, wheel-like revolvement. And the shining-up of it is the presentment of a solid surface. The electric, and still material ocean, holds all the infinitesimal particles in suspense. Further and further off, in the consideration of this dense thing, matter, and of still greater and greater tenuity, that is, atom-winnowing ; still no more than (to us and our senses, which are " we") the " point without parts and magnitude," the invisible spirit (still matter, although we are altogether incapable of it), comes the air, into which all matter escapes when we pursue it at the farthest, and drive it through the confines of our own world into that next. An elsewhere in which, when we say things are extinct, they have only taken refuge—flying to it as their next house.

Now this Elsewhere must be that containing all life next off this life, and be to us a life immortal, and the thing—as being beyond everything of us—divine, and taking in all to be supposed.

And farther. It has been the desire of man, in all ages, to penetrate to this something outside of him. It will never do to say that, by no trying, can we know it, and that we have nothing to do with it. A man, in his civilisation, might just as well express disregard concerning the next house in which he is to live. Though not come, it is to come. Though we have, at this present time, our own house about us, there will be another house, when we are out of this, in which we must still be. Now, in fact, the character of this other house, as it is to be so much more a lasting one, is of infinitely more consequence than the house in which man at present is. And which, as he knows all about and is familiar with, he takes no farther heed of. No farther heed of, than in regard of the due preparation and having at hand as of the "oil" indispensable to its maintenance, in order that, in the matter of his lamp, all doors may be shut against that possible and insupportable risk, the being left in the dark!

This carelessness about a present, and anxiety as to the oncoming lodging, is natural to the mind of man. Which ever seizes nothing of the present, but ceaselessly projects upon a future which, as it is uncertain, is therefore of the highest interest. So thought the Egyptians, who gave themselves almost altogether up to the thoughts of another life :—whose chief care, and most constant thought, was about the place in which they were hereafter to be ;—whose whole mind ran upon their sepulchre. This is as the answer to their gloomy philosophy.

It is clearly men's interest, if it were possible, and being so satisfied as they are with their present domicile and fearful of change (perhaps for the worse, only supposedly for the better), that their present habitation should be their whole, last, and only house. We cheerfully resign all the beautiful promises for the future, argue men in their secret minds (though no man dare to clothe his thoughts in words, even to his most intimate and reliable friend):—we will give up, and be glad to do so, all our hope—which we, as hypocrites, only call hope ; accusing ourselves of sins for form's sake, and, as it were, to " do the decent thing ;"—(as if we could deceive God !)—we will hand back the speculation about a future life other than and out of this pleasant body, if we could be guaranteed that there should be absolutely nothing for us when we fall asleep and pass unknowingly. And that, when we come to an end, there should be an end. Shakespeare, in Hamlet's converse with himself upon this subject, has embodied the whole story of man's secret thinking in regard of the keeping himself here. Utterly a coward, if he could be given back his dreads by that watching Exterior Power, he would willingly bargain for a fall of the curtain upon the drama of his life ; and want—nay, desire there not to be, by any means—an after " rise," and a next-coming act. In his great, mean selfishness—so base, so unhopeful, and

so untrustful is his nature—man would rather end
where he might end. And, having had his fill, or as
much as he could contrive to realise, of his pleasures
and his profits—nay, of his life of breath in this body,
and of the motion of his limbs and of the treats of his
senses—close his account, and say, Here let all end,
since my known world ends! Let me be of the future
as not of it, and let there be no farther ME—to take
the chances of that ME! In short, with Ophelia would
he say :—

"*I know what I am. But I know not what I may
be!*"

And that, as the character of that which I may be
must, of necessity, be chance :—aye, though even nine-
teen-twentieths of that chance shall be prosperous and
profitable to me!—yet, for the sake of that little
nineteen to one-twentieth, will I give up all my other
numerous and over-balancing chances, and be content
—nay, happy—to be put a stop to, and to be no more
I. No more a unit to be carried over as into the next
folio of figures, and to be bandied amidst the chances
of subtraction, multiplication, addition and division,
making the four kingdoms of that "overleaf" world
of arithmetic, or of the future. So little will we trust
God.

And yet, here we act with the clear light of the
best reason. Here we act with common-sense. The
above argument is the soundest that can be adduced
by the safest and the mightiest in his truths and his
statistics, Accountant-General. Nothing shall exceed
it by the rule of square. But what are your truths
and your conclusions? There they are; perfect; not

to be contradicted ; the most comfortable, and secure, and consolatory. Men, walking upon these lines of exactness, upon these solidly-true laws, would live a thousand years, or as long as they like. The world has been busy making rules for the world, ever since the world began. And yet, in all great objects, it is none the better for them. For what is there that, in a single word, tumbles all the top, upsets this whole network of proper things—this built-work of econo-mics, striking its foundations so deep down in essen-tial world's-truth ? What is there, that, imported into this microcosm of man, is, to that microcosm, and (in it) the whole spring that sets the puppets playing, in their own little world, as in an independent world? Men recognising the machinery, and thinking it their own, and of themselves, though God (the outside contriver) has supplied it all ? It is this fancied state of the self-sitting (at the centre) to the machinery, and it is the apparent meddling and the making with it, the supposed necessity of acting, and the felt (as far as man feels) necessity of acting. In other words, it is the imagined Free-Will, through which Deity works, raising up, in man's mind, the conviction of responsibility which (as far as his being extends) is undoubtedly responsibility ; but certainly is respon-sibility no farther than it.

What is there that contradicts, and sets at nought, all of the world—all the work of the world ? World-work as, from its guards and sureties, to defy the very non-agreeing Exterior Powers (meanwhile shaking the head at it) to break it up. Why, the poor little word is Volition ; without which the whole moves not. And, in that Will of Man, the Archangels have their lever, whereby they shall topple all his most conceited, loftiest, and most architecturally fashioned and solidest world's-buildings, and hurl them :—his mathematical webs, or his Babel—and him, their spinner and maker, outside, again, into the huge, pitiless, and know-nothing Unknown. Volition is as the little trap through which pass the strings to the hand that moves the puppets. It is as the little brass-hook in the head of all of them. Therefore man does (somewhat frequently) not the things which, by his own wise world-laws, he ought to do, and that most are expected of him. In fact, he does *other things*, and not the things which he meant. Which former things are of God. Upon his chalked lines of proposal, God, through man's will, walks the proposer as the Disposer. Volition asks not conduct out of man's book, but man accepts it against himself because he cannot help it. Imported that chance, in the affairs of the world, which works through the human volition (which thinks it acts while it is acted), all the world-laws, and all men's laws, are changed, and we are, all, that outside which writes the world, though we think ourselves the pen. We are indeed as pens, writing ourselves, in the hands of God.

The passions, affections, the bias, whim and unaccountable wildness of man, his caprices and his contradictions, make havoc of all his fine-balanced laws. If man were a pendulum, he would beat true seconds. But he has a knob of brass—self-moving—in his head. And it is seized with strange whimsies of going. The brass knob plays the true time on the

wires of the world. That which we see, in after
years, as absurd, but, at the time, thought the perfectest sense ; that which one could not avoid doing,
because we gratified ourselves, and " did ourselves"
in doing it—was the play or action of the unseen
POWER, working to an end of which we gathered not
an idea, nor which end we can see, now. But which
was assuredly the true end. But which, beyond all
doubt, could not have been any other. We are
moved, whether we like it or not. We do those
things which are appointed, because we cannot do any
other. It is by the shutting-out of the sight of other
things, that we do the one thing. Because we are IT
for a time. With all to alarm, with all to avert, with
all to warn, with all to deter, with all to render it
just the very thing which we should *not* do, why do
we a thing? Why, when it is against reason and
common-sense, and world's laws, and opposed to the
proprieties of the world, and of us ;—why, when there
is everything against it, do we enter upon anything?
Simply because, like a ship, we answer the HAND
which is upon our helm. Just because we obey a
universal spiritually magnetic law, which is not only
" itself," but us, also. Just because, in short, we are
true to ourselves. Thus we discover ourselves as
machines, mistaking that UNKNOWN THING, which acts
in us, for ourselves. Thus we find that our bodies
are only walking shows. While the exemplification
of the great outside life is, only, we. That, in fact, *we
are that great outside*, found for itself.

These things are difficult to understand. But they
are the basis of the mysticism of the East. Very

frequently, when we condemn assertions, made in the philosophy of the mystical Orientals, as preposterous, it is, in most numerous instances, ourselves only that are foolish in mistaking the true thing for which the sophists contend. If we were to find ourselves time to examine the nice distinctions, and the subtle statements, of the ancient arguers, we should continually find that, in the first place, we could not contradict, and, in the next, that we must admit positions which, at the first consideration of them, are altogether inconceivable. If men are too occupied either to attend at all to it, or to take any pains to acquire notions of philosophy, they should be content to take matters a little upon trust, and to leave abstruse questions in the custody, and to the interpretation, of those accustomed, by long habit, to them. They should, at least, respect those who, by no particular seeking of their own other than in the natural bias towards them, but simply through the natural gift, have devoted abounding time to the examination of evading, but the only reliable truths.

CHAPTER IX.

PHILOSOPHIC INQUEST INTO MATTER.

GRANTING that the querist seeks to pierce and to penetrate through all solid nature until he comes fairly out at the other side, as it were. Having detected and got behind nature, and seen it on the other side, he will have come upon nothing. He will, then, have transcended through all the known, and volatilised himself "into no soul." He is told that there is a *substratum* in which all things inhere, and without which things cannot be even supposed. And he has resolved to conquer down to this occult, slipping something—perpetually evading him (in his pursuit of it), of sense. Nature will seem to perform a certain mocking dance (in a circle) around him, in order, as with her laughter, to baffle his determined, and, at last, his desperate efforts. Breaking through ; to escape out of her embrace is impossible. The ring of shows will spin its delusions around him, perpetually making him as the centre, and keeping him, for his own sake—that is, for his existence sake—as the middlemost point. The wheeling panorama, above, below, and on either hand, encloseth him. And seeketh always to make him the centre of itself. It revolveth with incredible swiftness. If, in his force, he breaks the immediately outer-to-him circumvolvement :—if he, even, shall dive deeper and deeper (in his mind-power) through these fractured rings, they

close only, the next instant, before him the tighter, in
order that he may be, *himself*, maintained.   And his
extrication becomes all the more a difficult matter
as his constant day's experiences drive him farther
down into themselves.   So long as he is man, he
must move encumbered with these sensual rings. Each
is of a kingdom of experiences.   Baser, and denser,
and more and more of earth-thickness as he is more
of the world—owns more and more of the solid, of
the materially true, and of the every day, common-
place-undoubtedness, the more he is man, the less he is
other than man.   As the less is he other than a machine.

But, in his search after this hard thing, matter, he
takes the earth, and he still the finer and finer pulve-
rises it.   He gains in quantity what he loses in mass.
He moves from the one—the unity—*solid*, to the
number *parts*.   He has, now, quantity, but not solidity.
Forms have changed, but there is nothing other than
there was before.   As it were, he has only changed
the boards of his floor, but he has not reached his
floor.   He sets to work upon the departments of
nature.   He determines to submit all the machinery
about him to trial.   He resolves to pursue this flying
thing, matter, and to tear the mask from before its
ever-evading face.   He will conjure this Phantom into
his man's circle, and bid it speak.

He fells the trees; he reaps his harvests; he plucks
his flowers; he tears the larger and the lesser plants
from the bosom of their mother, Earth; he rives the
spiring, knotty trunks; he splits the scarcely wedgeable
blocks; he loosens and tumbles fragments from the
rugged, hoary mountain-side; he digs up the metal-

ore, and he strikes it with his instruments of striking, to get out of it that final binding thing, of which he is told, called MATTER, and to lay the secret creature bare. So that he may have it face to face with him. But what—after all—does he effect in these operations? What is that RESULT for which all the world clamours? In his acts of piecemeal·separation he has only *multiplied*, instead of reduced. He has only exerted farther and farther outwards, when the task which he has set himself has been to work farther and farther inwards. Matter is still unchanged.

He examines things, and thinks about things, to see if he can discover the occult means of their composition :—to spy into the secret laboratories of nature, and to find out in what manner she has been fluent— and what she has at the heart of all. He urges, in *some* fashion, to light upon the secret of her wheels. In what manner she has hardened her waves—closed up her walls—shut out the seeker from that last and ultimate thing on which is *inlaid all*—on which is painted all—according to his own philosophies. Which are the very philosophies that we deny have any foundation. For they have only come out of *him*.

The fibrous substances have intertwined and woven up themselves. They cling in lines. They twist in ropy convolution. They lay together, they spire together. Theirs is a brotherhood of affinities in which the fibrous lines shoot parallel. In the knots and cross-winding still is the force direct, though circumvolved. This is the manner in which the trunks of trees slowly labour up ;—the slower, the higher, and the more enduring they become. The stems of the lighter trees start the more saliently—boast a freer, fresher, and the livelier growth. A parallel radiation takes place in the form of branches. A thinning, and dividing, and alternating of the vital force. An insinuating, and winding, and veinwork-development, as it were, carrying about the blood in the guise of sap. The tree-like current, electrically spreads, in the medium of the thin air, by a like (though an opposite) process to the multiplication and spreading of the dense and solid metal-veins in the lighter and less compressed fields of the earths, and in the kindred, but less resplendently close, medium of the stones. A finer network, as a finer and more delicate microcosm, are the vascular tissues and the vegetable webs of the leaves of trees and plants, from the close-packed buds where lie, folded, little green kingdoms of expansion, and of winning, out of new states, in the times, as yet, not. As yet not, at least, to *them*.

The flowers are expansions;—fibrous "feelings," as it were, of the highest and lightest;—vegetable crystallisation (if there could be—at least explainable in words—such form in nature); yielding the life of themselves, as perfume, agreeable to human sense. For the lower animals have no sense of the odour of flowers, or, perhaps, have an anti-sympathetic and repellant one. The superflux, and spreading, and beauty of the fibrous, electric coating of the world, intensifying, in the hidden gift, into starlike radiation; into flights of microscopically beautiful—natural *fireworks*, if we may use so bold and strange a figure to express flowers. The beautiful forms of flowers, their so happy arrangement and disposition, their graceful curls, bells, and pendants; their spots, stars, dots, fringes, and ornaments; their shades, touches of bloom, varyings of texture; their glancing, dropping or hanging, waving, birth, life, and death; rising, spreading, radiating, unfolding, evolvement, seeding, disintegration or falling to pieces, are the triumph of the instinct-life; of fecund, almost *over-living* matter, worked-up and manufactured-up—if we may introduce such a word—as if by fairy hands, into glory.

The flowers are the children of the fields; the miniature populace of the kingdoms of the woods, and the lawns, and the hollows. They are the last settlements and resolutions of the unseen, microscopical, electric world-force :—as the golden fringe to the great purple pall of matter. What their colours—apart from the inappreciably delicate affections of the eye that sees them, of the intelligence that finds them in its sense-feeling—are, who shall discover? What is their perfume but the infinitesimally minute dissipation of themselves?—their more powerful, or the weaker, according to the atmospherical conditions, generation of themselves? their steady breathing, tranquil in the quietness of nature? What is the scent of these multicoloured, inexpressibly beautiful, fairy flocks of flowers—these chaliced troops—this jewellery of the great fiery-gold summer—these squadrons of glittering *daylight* torches?—if they, the torches, could be so borne and be so innumerous! What, we reiterate— in the sense of the arch-chemists of the Paracelsian or Rosicrucian school—is the perfume of flowers, but their slow, unfiery combustion?—or decay, or death,

perhaps—in the vital heats. Flameless, in the acceptation of sense, to *realise flame*, and, yet, flame, of its
kind, to other gifts to find it? Burning, into dissipation, in other sense than that mere human sense, which
makes heat (as felt by man) its measure and the means
of its detection. For perceived heat is only *evolution*,
as passing through man's method of knowing it.

Physical heat—by which we mean fiery heat—and
moral heat, are not so dissimilar as people suppose.
The heat of the mind is a forceful agitation, akin to
the real material heat. Since it dissipates, and forces
objects apart, and into new forms. But it has no
flame, whereby the bodily eye shall descry it. And
we are fools if we limit things by our bodily senses,
which are nothing, except in the things intended for
them. The things of the mind may have their spiritual
flame. The glory of the mind may be a glory of
light, just as world's things burn in real fire, and as
material objects shine in "eyelike" light. Both being,
after all, only *agitations*. The one real, to the body's
regard; the other, just as real to another power,
unknown of sense;—namely, the sight of the soul.

Flowers are the best proof of the gracefulness, and
beauty, and innate splendour of the possibilities of
matter. For they are its culmination; the highest it
can do—the most it can effect—towards the light,
refined, beautiful, and the perfect. It is the attenua-
tion and glory, through the fragility, as it were, of the
spirits of matter:—this starring, and spotting, and
speckling in the light-woven outer spheres, or *media*, of
matter, or of "mass-sympathy to itself." Flowers are
as the breaking of nature into beauty—like a daybreak.

And are not men vain—and, indeed, philosophers wrong—in talking of this thing gravitation, or gravity, or weight, as a thing real? They ought to know that it is only *measureless sympathy.* That this attraction is only the reaching-out of matter—as with arms—to embrace itself. That weight is only a mere figment; and that we only mistake the universal *taking into itself to keep out the outside*—the weaving-up of itself— the spreading of matter—the magnetic *synthesis* because you cannot thrust in anything between—for a some- thing of itself. Gravity is the insisting grasp of the real, to itself. Out of it, is generated a world. It is the closing together, except for that other thing— *more of itself*—to prevent. In short, gravity is universal magnetic attraction: there being no such thing as weight. Gravity is the clockwork of the world. Gravity is as the chart on which the world is written.

The clinging-together, and the hold—so tight— that matter has of itself, is to be insinuated into un- loosing, or melted, or untwined, or struck out and overcome, if we would take this world, as it were, to pieces, and discover what secret evading thing it is that makes it. And that it has behind.

We must set to work, with our anatomy, not to discover formation, for that we know already in chemistry, geology, and all the other kindred " making-up," real and sensible sciences, but to get at the soul—if we so can. This, indeed, has ever been the aim of the greatest philosophers, up to whose labours—as servants of them—all the other querists of nature worked. Thence came the exalted name, Alchemist—as the prince, or master, or arch-priest of chemists. Having exhausted all the departments of natural philosophy—having put by, as it were, into memory, and searched through in experiment all that could be told in the accumulation of the chemists or the anatomists of matter—the grand master-chemist, or Alchemist, gathered up all the figures, as we may say, into *sums*, and worked products of them. Seeing, as it were, the consummated and immortal beauty, and the great truths, and the hypernatural laws in the wondrous building. The component parts, or fragments, or stones of which the meaner artists and merely mechanical workers (as builders to him, the architect) gathered up painstaking, though unknowingly, for his divine dealing—his magical and disbelieved (of men) handling of them.

The Philosopher's "Stone" we, perhaps, believe to mean the magic mirror, or translucent spirit-seeing crystal, in which imposssible-seeming things are disclosed. The *menstruum*, or universal dissolvent, a transmuting element, the *elixir vitæ* or a power of general regeneration, magical means in their widest sense—a capacity to deal with the materials of nature until quite contrary things are evolved of them:— every phase of impossible knowledge has been assumed of these philosophers. That soon, outside of our material nature, the grand lights begin to shine, was their argument. But by the vulgar their accomplishments were suspected as the forbidden golden keys of the very treasure-house in which lie the means of unlocking the gates to the immortal knowledge.

We, with the other Immaterialists, hold that this secret and unknown thing which makes the world, is only the law which makes it. We dispense with, and deny, all medium, or matter, or occult substance in which, and on which, things are to be. And which is to be compounded-up and spelt out of, to make them. We hold, metaphysically, that there is no such thing as matter. That it is a mere miserable, unsound-of-mind, poverty-stricken, childish figment, conjured up out of the incapacity of men's thinkings. We maintain that that which on indisputable evidence —the contrary of it being contradiction, or madness, or impossibility, or, worse than impossibility (because impossibility and something else)—cannot be, is to be rejected with indignation and opprobrium, expelled with laughter, met with the anger at an attempted deceit, as not, in any way, being. We consider the world as made only as a thing in the acceptance of it in the unconsciousness of the senses ; as furnished in the life in which it is only found. And we take that unconsciousness as the true man's state and the true world, the man being then not himself, but just the things outside of him. To take away which, would be to take *him*.

In this sense—and we believe it is the true—man's life is as a continual dream, no way worthier than any other dream. No more a thing than a picture. And human as any life is nothing other than made in itself, and out of the vividness of the sense-things. In these sense-things man is, and he and they (or the identity) are only vivid, that is, real, and—in seeming—*all*, as they come out, and are the produce, of the exertion of the bodily faculties, or the man. No more true and substantially real, we repeat, than the sleep-dreams in which the man (out of this life) leads all sorts of lives. And sound lives, too, in their way, apart from the life of his body, which is mechanism!—and no less true, committed to other balances to be weighed. The memory of the past years, the flitting of objects, the things recalled in our world of bygones, is—carefully looked-at, and abstractedly looked-at—of the same stuff as are dreams. We mean, that that which we call our real life is a panorama in us, that is " supposedly" out of us. But, in the world, we, of course, admit real world.

Endeavour to recall a place, or person, seen in the past, and we find the image much of the same difficult, unlike, shadowy, and unbelieved character as the things of dreams. All that makes memory consistent, and a real chain of things, is the infinite linking of small sensations, down from the particular large or little matter remembered, to this moment present. It is a long telegraphic, where the signals are caught up from one idea to the other. The links of the long chain, in memory, are temporarily lost hold of, and the two ends are that only which connects. Like, too, as of the telegraph, it is only the sender and receiver that are in communication.

We cannot tell wherefore, or how, we recognise, in the world, a face long lost sight of. But the recall of it is effected, and in an instantaneously unconscious act of magic command and instant show in answer, after, perhaps, one or two very wide, and dreamlike, and baffled enforcements, or striking on the outside world of figures, resemblances, and objects, ordering the particular *slinking* idea forth! The revival is as that of a mere dream. And the face of a forgotten, or not-thought-of person, as it were, is shown up in the magic-lantern of our memory, as caught, or observed, or printed at a particular moment of past time to us. Respecting the whole scene of which we can give no account, other than that it was something which struck us from the most trifling, dreamlike, and absurd reason, perhaps, in the world. It is as in a dream-glance that we remember most things, when we are not soliciting forcibly towards them. And, in exercising our attention, we bring in the faculties of the mind, and therefore a portion of our body's history, in common experience. Places and things remembered are not the places and things. Nothing like them. They pale and retire off like a phantom. They become merely a picture. They are inconsistent and absurd—they seem to swim—when sought to be put at any distance from us for the purpose of being examined, by themselves, in the mind's view, and struck from association in the non-essential to life, analysis. Let our reader try at this sort of curious personal experiment. Taking out an Idea from its world of association, let him endeavour to examine its face steadily by itself, so that he may know his friend again. He will experience a singular and new effect of the mind-optics, which will let in abundance of suggestion towards this apparently—but only apparently—inexplicable dogma of the metaphysical non-reality of things. Let it be always remembered that the thinker must, in every instance, extricate himself from these things, before—out of them—he can see them as "clothes"—now nothing—out of which he has stepped. In them, they are real enough, and full of purpose enough, to everybody. It is the chains that make the prisoner. Out of them the man is not held.

Other than in their necessity of seeming to us, things are not. Philosophical analysis proves that this must be so. Just as there is no time out of the clock that measures it.

If the views, and if the things in dreams had the same bodily organs—for they *have* organs of their own—in other words, a sky to their world—to take them up; the same mechanism to make sense out of them, the same magic-lantern sort of apparatus in which to catch shows, and to cause them to remain as in the life-body, what is there to prevent them being as real, and as true, as the matters in this every day world? Time and Space being things necessary for man, seem, to us, to be the cause (and almost, if not all, the cause) of the difference. The lower animals have no Time and Space, but only an intuition in the place of both. In other words, they move as in the assurance and certainties of dreams, where all is, because it is, and nobody questions—nor is there anybody *to* question! How *we* should seem to the animals is, indeed, a strange thought. But speculation on this head, just now, would lead us out of our way. Infinitely more lies under this, though, than is supposed.

We will show that it is only this Time, and this Space, (which every thinker knows to be nothing,) that make the world. And surely if that which makes a thing be nothing, the thing must be nothing.

Strike out all the spaces and the stops of a page of type, and get some sense out of it! Yet there are the letters, and there is the sense, if you import but one condition into it. Time is necessary to measure man out. But a man in dreams is a non-natural man. And his dreams being not necessary to him, and nothing of him as MAN, he—though the things may be real—has no time in them. Therefore are they as the unspaced page of type. Things without sense—a huddle of letters;—with reference to the sense of language—only to laugh at!

Nature never gives that and more. It never does that which is unnecessary. It first does the thing. Now Time and Space are indispensable to man. They make him. And he cannot be made without them. But, as man is not man in the dream-state, and as that world of dreams—however true it may be to itself—has no truth in the world of man's certainties, and has nothing to do with his life, it being altogether irregular and anomalous, a miracle, and *something else*, therefore Time and Space could be of no value and meaning in it, as not being wanting to make it:—the man being not to be made in it. And, therefore, they are not there. And it is this very fact of Time and Space being taken out of it, that alone makes the absurdity of dream-life. That being wise and real enough to the sleeper, if recalled at all, (which it is very rarely,) being mad, and wild, and of no significance—save through feelings which he imports—sometimes a perplexing, and, yet, unaccountable cargo—into his day-state—to the fully-awake man, with his, then, new—but his true, because he has a body and senses—world, come about him so welcomely again!

And there is absurdity in the popular thoughts about dreams. As they are so common, nobody enquires about them. And nature, doubtless, meant them (in the low phases through which this world passes) not to be understood commonly, in order that the world's business should not be interfered with, or interrupted. Rightly looked at, that veil which hangs over to-morrow is a direct miracle. For the future must be just as distinct, just as much already acted, just as much a matter settled and accomplished, just as much past, as the real past. Day by day, the veil of the future is lifted by the POWER outside us. *And we have walked on into " next days."* A farther and farther " pair of houses," on each side, as it were, we have " come parallel to," as our spiritual feet have stept, or obtained, to us more and more—a day's instalment—out of that shadowy *street* of the "morrow." But the " whole street" is there, at this moment, disclosed to *another sight*. Though we, only, are aware, in our own bodily knowledge, of our achieved portion of it. Thus, of real, time, man gains not a jot. Nothing of the future is made for him. It is all there, though he does not know it. The pavement is spread for him, though, step by step, he has his own flags. And all his accidents are there waiting for him. Visorred ministers whose ghostly beavers are only to be lifted, and the sight of them as a human face, to be disclosed, when he steps up face to face with them. His events are there, though he must come up to them, for them to arise as monuments, silently, to him out of the ground. And all these chances—bad or good—may be diverted, as into the way of another man. In his own Free-Will, he may turn up another street. But it is the shadow, cast by the Unseen across his path, that has induced him to it. And, in the magic of fatality which has nothing of his miserable necessities, his whole (now changed) perfected "street of chances," bound by no laws of *his* world, has curved, and slided, as it were, to meet his feet, giving another scene, in the new-chosen direction :—another street and the same ! Since it is only in the *descent to him* that the change has been made. But, *upwards to God*, it has been that which it always was. God being unchangeable.

Now, as knowledge of the future is only denied to man AS MAN, and his ignorance of it is necessary to make him, since, if he knew the future, his life would be already *past*, and he would make no move-ment towards that which he already knew (or was), therefore, when man ceases to be man—all revela-tion, or impossibility, being sure to be disbelieved, as not of it, *when he comes back into his body-state :—* glimpses of the forward world, and of the REAL world outside his show-world, may happen. Man must not pull his house to pieces, in order that he may live in it ! In order that he may have the roof of his human-nature over him. His windows must be closed, and he must sit with his single small candle (since, to be at all, he must live in his own light). He must be closed-up, and live, alone, in his own house of senses, to make him that which God intended he should be in this world. As man must be in a "state," he must not realise any other state. Else, as the small renders into the larger, the concrete "drop" flows into the unbodied "water." He must be like a man moving in his house, with closed windows, by candle-light, we repeat, while the unsuspected great radiance of the sun is shining without. His self-contained, candle-lighted darkness must be maintained, to make him man. For to throw open his windows, and let in the noonday sunshine, would be to kill the candle (himself). And human intelligence, and God's Knowledge, cannot co-exist. For one destroys the other. The candle is put out by the sun.

Great nature's secrets are at the safest in being disbelieved. They are so intended. Impossibility makes the world. For impossibility once believed in, the world would cease. The truth of these things is obvious, and a little consideration brings about the free assent to them. The positive and negative poles of a magnet are both equally true; but only at their own ends. We dare as well declare that man cannot be when we see him without his chains, as that we should be correct in calling him a free man when we behold him bound. And yet the man is the same. His states are equally true. So with the dreamer. He is in other worlds, as true, of their kind, as our world. Only, now he is in the one, and not in the other. If it could be possible to put questions to him in the dream-state, his answers would be satisfactory enough. But we have no means of access to him in that state. Being, ourselves, not in "fellow-dreams," or in his strange world, and only in our own. As it were, thus :—Greek to his Hebrew; both being *lan-*

guages; he and ourselves, however, only knowing our own.

The *phantasmagoria* of real things are probably presented, as with glasses ill adjusted—in the magic-lantern of our sleeping brain. The perspectives are but irregularly projected—perhaps that is all. Dreams are as the dark sides of the lighted forms of the things of the world. Those shadowy (but with torchlight-illumined) visages—those forms *umbered* in the mystery of that half-world, or no world, of which they are the only witness, are as striking (because as wonderful) as sparks, for flowers, speckling a dark Eden! Even the moon—queen of the darker realm—may not disclose the placid, yet slumbrous beauty of those visionary intelligences who wait in darkness. The darker angels—angels of the silent night—theirs is but the melancholy loveliness—a woe-begone sublimity—floated to apprehension out of the whole depth of the Unseen! That blank in which ye brood to view, ye living Dreams! is, as it were, a voiceless twilight, in which ye are rather *suggested*, than appear to move. Ah holy, though so dark a Land of Dreams!—thou country without sound, though busy with a thousand feet!—the dusky Cherubim are those, alone, to guard thy mystic splendours. Thou land, shadowless with clouds in that one great cloud; —thou country so thickly starred, yet, with stars, unilluminate ;—thou realm so populous, and, yet, of life so empty ;—thou so-royal Kingdom, all void but with the ill-according hints of that so proudly true and so little suspected, the nameless presences are those, alone, that guard that DOOR OF SLEEP, through which, as out of our day-life, or real life, into night-life, we pass to thee !

We wish it to be clearly understood that in the preceding philosophical disquisition, and especially in the advancing of such strange and, apparently, unbelievable opinions, we are only endeavouring to give an abstract view of the peculiar doctrines and reveries of the mystic Buddhists, and of their successors in the more modern day—though these are old enough ! —the Rosicrucians. That all these ideas are based upon the conclusions which natural philosophy and science afford, and that, however remarkable, they are not to be contradicted—following as they do the natural sequence of the metaphysical (which is the last) logic—is a truth that will be a satisfaction to the mind, though the assent may not be as fully—or, indeed, at all—given. In exhausting the examination of nature, we can alone come upon these bases— shadowy, as they seem, out of all that is of man. We are not responsible that the devious paths of knowledge lead as to a country so airy. Though, unmistakeably, they have the advantage of conducting from all denseness and materialism. Opposed to which is the whole object of our book. For we seem to recognise that it is in the gulf of materialism that the loss of religion, in the modern days, is threatened. Men's thoughts, business, inquest, treasures, conquests, life, are all too much of the world. Compliance with our present position, and fear—or no thought of it at all— are the great enemies of religious inquiry. But men are beginning to grow restless and wiser !

CHAPTER X.

VALUE OF TRADITION.

WE believe that the universal attestation and impressions of antiquity are just as of equal validity, and as much things to be accepted, as history. Tradition is not a thing of childish credit. It is hoar as old age itself. It is a vain and a wrong thing, to talk of the infancy of the world. Its infancy has only lain in its ignorance of the methods and means of smoothing its existence here. Surely life is something more than the knowledge of how to make ourselves comfortable in it. Yet, this is all that man's accumulated modern knowledge—including all his science—amounts to.

Science—world's knowledge—is only conversant with adaptation to a given state :—which state is alone relation, and which philosophy can prove to be nothing. The utmost capacity of man's mind—all that is found—was as perfect in the first thinker as in the highest civilised individual ; whose very soul has grown back into " things" through the huddle of world-furniture in which his mind is enveloped—nay, which makes his mind. That which we call life is world's experiences, written one over the other, from the child up and through the man ; the earliest disappearing.

In rhapsody, in those moments wherein we are

taken out of ourselves, at those times when the investitures are torn from the living soul; in its storm and in its disturbance, when the necessities of this world of senses no longer close it in, at birth ere they come, and before death, when those scenes of senses go, and when the hinges are breaking (from the pressure into freedom of the liberated spirit, shattering in triumph its no-longer-needed cincture), then do the eternal rays strike down. Then it is, when things go because no longer wanting, the man ceasing; then it is that irruption is made and storming effected, back, down, into and upon our first writings upon ourselves—our first scenes of this life:—life alone—again in the Buddhist view—of accumulated *layers* of *phantasmata*. Spirit-light breaks in upon our charnel of flesh. The flesh of which Black Deaths alone is the King. And He again—that Death—is but the change over, or convulsion, into new being; painful only in the retrogression, but not in the advance. Death being insensible birth. Man, because he is man and not child, is therefore away from the Great Truth:—that from which the child comes the freshest.

Therefore, was Novalis right, who says that:—
" Children are the first men. They are fresh from truth. Little Souls let out from God's sky. And they come—with their small sensations—with amazed eyes, strange and wondering, out of their own world into this new world. They are as waking up and rubbing their eyes to new sense-solicitations. Or rather are they not as falling asleep, in this world, and coming asleep to us, as into the dark, with their fondling, trustful fingers, as out of their own light

world! Thus to the child—until reassured amidst the shadows of the hands of those to whom he is dear—all is at first Terror. Terror which is the first thing—and 'before the Gods'—which men find. The first man is the first spirit-seer. All appears to him as spirit. What are children but first men? The fresh gaze of the child, with all the bloom of the immortal worlds upon him, is richer in significance than the forecasting—like a demi-god—of the philosopher, world-old in almost supernatural Knowledge." "But in the wearisome noise and petty conflicts of contending modern Theologies," so says Carlyle, "the history of man, as of the child, is not a mighty drama enacted in the theatre of Infinity, with Suns for lamps and Eternity as a background; whose author is God, and whose purport and thousand-fold moral lead us up to the 'dark with excess of light' of the Throne of God, but a poor, vexatious, dull, debating-club dispute spun through the hollow centuries."

And therefore world-knowledge is not so worthy as child-intuition.

CHAPTER XI.

THE PHILOSOPHIC SCHEME OF LIFE.

NATURE has provided two cradles for her great child, man—the cradle proper, and the coffin. Our original cradle is white, and our last one is black. And that is nearly all the difference. Their is a *noise* between, and that is all. Old women officiate at our entrance into life. They also speed us at our departure from it. It is, therefore, a mean thing at both ends. The phenomena are infant-like at birth and at death. How much they are so has scarcely ever yet inspired observation. Our necessities shrink to the meanest at the beginning and at the end of our time. Our glory is about as great when we retire from it as when we enter upon the grand drawing-room of life. We are poor candles that are to burn a certain time in the wind; and then, with a puff, that *which men saw* is gone. And whither? The jewel is tossed out, and we have the rotten setting. Watch-wheels without that which comprises them into watch; the bag with the string run out and snatched away;—the writing without the means to read it;—the horse without the back upon which to mount. We begin with the rattle; and end, indeed, with another kind of rattle. Grim similitude! But wholesome for our height of pride.

We commence with the spoon and end with the spade :—two domestic and almost as equally useful

implements, of which the only difference seems that
the one is to be used within the house, and the other
without.   We come noisily.   But we go out silently.
As shadows pass along a wall, so we gain the
knowledge that whole generations at all were, but
by a certain something resembling lamplight.   As
wise would it be to send some one to gather up the
shadows when the lamp is carried away, as to look for
these human shows of the past in the blank of the
present.

O, unhappy man, and most mistaken shadow!
perpetually purporting to yourself to be certainly not
that which you are; for all the real sense that you
have of your life, you lived long ago.

Life is the enigma of which death is the answer.
Death, seen through the true spectacles, is the seed
to which life runs.   It is only as the difference or
change over from one life into another.   Thence the
pain.   The war is only with the remaining elements.
Before, all is the easy way.   Dissolution is the fruit
of life to which the plant runs, and on the other hand,
"Life never dies;—*matter dies off it.*"

All life is a profuse and impulsive growth.   Matter
teems, pulsates, and rings in its vital energy.   All
forms of vitality are an electric sprouting.   From the
very centre of the starting mass—from the heart of
the globe—by an unseen sort of self-excrcitation the
forces radiate.   The round of articulations is the restless fruitage of pregnant nature.   Trees, bushes, and
plants are a mathematical electric efflux.   They stretch,
they spire, they spring in starry figure; they knot, they
weave, and they bind as in all the fantastic telegraphics

of the electric jets. Forms, of all kinds, are nature striving to express. Nature writes its meanings in its overgrowth; wreaks itself in shape. The innumerable forms of articulate nature are but started earth; "clay loosed, and under names." Shapes are the impulse of nature forced beyond its original bound by power unseen;—a dropped product;—a highly-wrought, organically active growth; the mechanic concentration up and inwardly to a point, and then the spreading fitness to certain new conditions. Locomotive life is the independent and fructified perfectness.

As the apex and end of this grand tree-like intensification and superfecundity, and as the triumph of the *Flora*, we behold man. In all his mechanic glory, in all his "vegetable" laws, he is nature's primest self-assertion. Knit in one common origin with, and compounded and made up of the self-same congregate and restless atoms as the feeblest of the universal efflorescence, his brethren are the plants. His bases—chemically changed—are as their bases.

Thus allied, by the myriad ramifying links, to the universal growth and life bursting out all over the world, man himself, in his ultimate disentanglement from the *limbo* of earth-forms, may be correctly regarded, even, but as the " disengaged and locomotive vegetable !"

Why then may not all vegetative articulation—trees electrically spread and ramified—including man with his arms as branches and his hands as leaves, his stomach as the congeries of roots, and his legs as tentacles—the self-moved or migratory "plant," as it were;—why may not this whole round of tree-like overgrowth be as a microscopic show in a fecund medium; thick in matter, which is the refuse, and lees, and " cloud-groundwork," as it were, of life. For all is as *a nebula*; seething, generating, germinating. Why may not all this mass of vegetative life—including man, as far as we know him (his soul being an intuition, being "God in us")—be forced, upward and outward, from out and off the surface of nature by moral density, gravity, and the superincumbent and propellent and forceful supervital downward (and then upward) impulse. As the tubed mercury declines in answer to the " upward" rise, and then rises in counterbalance to the " downward" pressure owing to the density, or gravity, or spreading-out, of that which we call atmosphere, or medium. This may even comply satisfactorily with the old mystic doctrine—the magnetic theories of Battista Van Helmont, Paracelsus, and the other magnetists. These theorists reiterated that the imprint, or show, of all things mundane, remain, as displayed forms or objects, after they have disappeared, and been utterly obliterated; not to be distinguished as far as the human sensibilities are capable of them. And that in the nature of things—having once existed—they must remain as long as matter remains.

Evidence from all times, from the most opposite quarters (wonderfully consonant and corroborative when judged deeply), concurs in insisting that there is, after all, some truth in the strange things told us. Truth though deformed in the means and methods through which it has arrived at us. That it should not agree with our experience is no proof, to a wider circle of experience, that it may not be known. Just as (though a thing may not even be, apparently, in conformity with common sense) that the thing may be nevertheless true when applied to, and produced by, another machine, no part of which resembles the first. Which is the mere simple adaptation only— means to end; "common sense" to "ordinary intelligence." As a "round" to the figure of a "circle," which, by the laws of its being, being a "circle," cannot be made to apprehend, nor, in the nature of things, can be comprehensive of a "square." We are contending for *relation* here; which is the whole being. Neither more nor less; but it.

Very properly are miracles rejected by the common sense of mankind. Man acts most like a man—that is, falsely; his standard of perfection being the standard of his identity with that which makes him, namely, relation—in repudiating that which is impossible to him.

But his reason has no reference except to that which makes it. It "sees down to a centre" when we call upon it to "work outward." Which it cannot do. The laws of all knowable things—all knowable things—are as "one to ten." Man is as "one to ten." Within from "ten inwards to one" he traverses his mortal capacity. Between those points is his reason. Because he is the contained, and not the container. How then shall he judge of "fifteen," when it is not within the capacity of him? Therefore shall it, to him, be a madness. Though as true as his own arbitrary numbers. This is true.

CHAPTER XII.

SLEEPING AND WAKING.

It is, perhaps, to be believed that, as man is the mere machine of the daylight, obeying the polar transference of day and night, that, in his sleep, a change-over is effected of the magnet which constitutes him. And that the sensitive and thinking point is transferred to the other pole; namely, his stomach. The change-over is effected, in the healthy human, in a totality so namelessly complete; and the fact, itself, is so beyond measure startling and, seemingly, wild, as, from the very lightning-like quickness of the change, still more from its apparent impossibility, to be the safest. That is, as all nature's greatest truths are at the safest—IN BEING DISBELIEVED. Though the strange facts may be none the less true. These things are not necessary for man's Knowledge. Whose very "perfectness of life" is his unconsciousness.

Many suspicions occur to the sage physiologist— whose researches have rendered him deep-seeing— that the above singular change-over should be, perhaps, true ; however little seemingly consistent. Magnetists and mesmerists, from cogent experiences, accept the probable reality of it. Some of the ablest men believe it. There are, indeed, a number of arguments and a formidable array of evidence—weighed with philosophical calmness and with acute insight:—and this

even notwithstanding our continually interfering pre-
judices, and the distorting science-lights in which we
lose real things.   Much should seem to attest as true
this strange operation of mysterious and wonderfully-
working Nature.   Head or stomach are incontestably
alike indifferent to that which needs neither, to be,
out of man;—that is, out of his natural state, or
waking state.   For the machine is left in its own
world, while the perception is taken elsewhere.   It
then exists by new laws.   Though at the sudden
alarm of its watchmen, the merely *suspended* Senses,
the whole castle of flesh may, by a rough figure, be
said to rally back and re-blaze with its human light.
Senses or faculties, like enlarged prisoners, summoned,
again, back within their bars, from the now, to them,
paled splendours of the immortal truths.   Brilliant
truths, thought, in the senses, feeblest-lighted dreams!

According to Dr. Ennemoser, one of the consequences of the very completeness of man, is a weak
and insufficient development of instinct.   And thus
the healthy waking, conscious man, is, of all organisms, the least sensible to the impressions of this
universal intercommunication and polarity.

" In sleep, and in sickness," he says, " the higher
animals, and man, fall, in a physico-organical point of
view, from their individual independence, or power
of self-sustainment.   And their polar relation—that
is, their relation to the healthy and waking man—
becomes changed from a positive to a negative one.
All men, in regard to each other, as well as all
nature, being the subject of this polarity."

Other physiologists, however, believe, from the

numerous and well-attested cases of the transference of the senses, in disease, to the pit of the stomach, that the activity of the brain, in sleep, *is* transferred to the epigastric region. The instances of this phenomenon, as related by Dr. Petetin and others, have been frequently published.

CHAPTER XIII.

PHILOSOPHY OF DREAMS.

WHAT is sleep? What is the need of it? Why do men sleep? Why, when the curtains of night are let down, does all nature—at least, all animated nature—experience that sense of the taking-away of the light? Why, if we were not (only) made out of the day, are we referred into the lower worlds, where we become impossible? Man, in his life, is only a middle thing. He is a gleam between two some-things, which are *him*, only, as he lives;—only back-wards and forwards of him. This should prove that his nature is nothing out of his sense-nature. And as his sense-nature is only that " before" and " after"—arrested, as man, in this world—he is only that before and after. This world being, only, as a sun-glance, downwards, out of the whole sunshine. A particular minute of Light—in this world—out of a whole day of it elsewhere. The evanescent water-floors of thought recede as from under us, departing and roll-ing down into the great ocean. We, once, were on these waves, and were in them, and occupied with the things which they produced about us. But they sink (as a sea), as below, from off our life's strand. And they leave but little, unregarded, and trivial matters, showing up, to us, as on the sea-beach when the tide goes down.

It is a strange thing, that, in memory, we recall matters by a suggestion through some trifle which helps on, only, the introduction of the greater idea. We obtain the thing we look for, only by the means of something which we did not look for. We only remember things by second means to them. And how singular is the play of the machinery of thinking! Some odd look, quirk, unlikely trifle, standing bodily up out of the *flat* (so to liken it) of the mind-picture; —something which has nothing to do with the thing, and is absurd, and as a non-consequence, in regard of it—is that which we find most distinctly fixed—most to leap up from, to sight. We remember a scene by a particular garment which a man has on who is a figure in it, the most inconsequential thing in the world, alone, to recall it by, and, yet, to its appearance, and in all appearance, the most natural in the world. And those whole things are most deeply remembered which are most wholly striking; most remarkable, and important, out of our daily life. The ordinary and the familiar are the stuff which may be unregarded, in the world of things, and may be consigned, into the universal gulf, as the material, in no manner more important than as the phases of the life here, or than as the supplying of the furniture of the masquerade of the man in this being. But the great events, which are as the rents and loopholes, in this world, through which the great, outside INVISIBLE looks in upon us, are as the signals and beckoning which bind us to man. Therefore they remain, though, being as less of the world, they ought not. And we regard this as some sort of shadowy, though forcible, proof of the *phantasmata* of this man's world. This human state of a cloud of sense-foldings, of which all its light and meaning is obtained from itself. A globe luminous, alone, from its centre.

And as in this life with our memories, so in the world of dreams—a proof of their following a certain fellow-like law, if we could but discover it—it is most the little absurd things, of seemingly no manner of, even, *irrational* connection with them, by which we recall scenes. It is upon a trifle, unwinding as a point for them to turn upon, or as a star for the magic fires to open themselves into spreading-out upon; it is, indeed, upon a little thing that all the mysteries, and all the strange stories, of our dreams revolve. That they expound, and to our senses, in the day-state, disclose to even the partial, and to the half-seized re-exhibition and second working of them, at any time or under any circumstances possible.

The universal, magnetic, emotional sense, or affection of body, only becomes sight when it enters into the delicate machinery (to the end of sight) in the eye; only is transformed, or made, into hearing, when it enters into the chambers of the ear; assumes the form whereby to know it, when it is taken upon the palate; commits itself, out of the intangible into the tangible, when it places itself within the power of the touch :— is tasted, touched, seen, felt; whatever we choose to call it, when man smells it. Thus all senses are *at one* outside of man and of physical being :—made, or spread out, to make *him*, or it. In dreams, we exercise all our senses without the machinery of sense.

We omit the wonderful effects upon the dreamer,

related of certain plants and animals, to remark that
"we be most given to dreams at spring and fall, also
when we lie with our face upward, but never grovelling."
(Nat. Hist. Plin., translated by Philemon Holland,
X., 175. Ib. xxviii. 4.)

The ascetic discipline, which usually introduces
to vision, in the general hallucinated sense, is only
necessary because the usual life of man is utterly contrary to the order of nature.

The first magician who is recorded as such, and
who gave distinct teaching on the subject of magic, is
Zoroaster. The genius of Socrates, of Plotin, Por-
phyrius, and Jamblichus, of Chichos and Scaliger, and
Cardanus, is placed in the first rank, which included
inward (magic) sight, and the motives of unusual
appearances. The dream was regarded as a universally natural gift, as a brother of death, teaching us
more of that unfettered vision and action which we
shall possess in the last sleep, when all these bolts and
bars are withdrawn, which, in sleep, are but loosened.
We refer to page 25 of the First Volume of Dr.
Ennemoser's History of Magic. Also to Robert Fludd,
who was the expounder of the theories, and the, in
so many respects, profound doctrine of the great mag-
netist, Paracelsus. Fludd, or Flood, wrote in 1638.

When two men approach each other, their magnetism is active or passive; that is, positive or negative.
If the emanations which they send out are broken or
thrown back, there arises antipathy, or *magnetismus
negativus*. But when the emanations pass through each
other from both sides, then there is positive magnetism;
for the rays proceed from the centre to the circum-

ference. In this case, they not only propagate sick-
nesses, but also moral sentiments. This magnetism, or
sympathy, is found not only amongst animals, but also
in plants, and prevails throughout the world. Every
day's experience is calculated to fortify these conclusions, which are strange, only, as not being usually
thought upon.

CHAPTER XIV.

MAGIC REVERIES OF ROSICRUCIANS AND BUDDHISTS.

IT is very striking, that, in all ages, all people have clothed the ideas of their dreams in the same imagery. It may, therefore, be asked, whether that language which now occupies so low a space in the estimation of men, be not the actually waking language of the higher regions, while we, awake as we fancy ourselves, may not be sunk in a sleep of many thousand years, or at least in the echo of their dreams, and only intelligibly catch a few dim words of that language of God, as sleepers do scattered expressions from the loud conversation of those around them. So says Schubert in his " Symbolism of Dreams."

That term, Sleep, is only a relative, and not an arbitrary term. Sleep, and the dreams which come in it, consist, only, of that stage, short of Death, which lies at the base of the pile of abstracted lives, out of our everyday life. Thus, the next state of abstraction, out of broad, waking, perfect sense-life, in which everything is exactly as we see it, is thought. Then comes revery, or absorption, in which we fall, again, a stage into the invisible; (but, yet, true—though as true elsewhere, though not about us). Then succeeds deeper absorption, in which the God-gift, Imagination, sees things. And, indeed, only *recovers* things when it is thought to be the making of things. This latter gaining is, however, only (so to say) the acquisition of new wealth out of old worlds; —the importing of the riches of one time into another time. To this supervenes vision;—absence in other places;—conjuring of other scenes;—new senses of deeper and wider working;—greater command upon the Unseen;—day-dreams, in which state of perfect quiescence (to be capable of them), where the mind is surrendered up, as a clear glass, ready for outside images to reflect upon, shows of the magical world roll in. There is every form of the dream-state, from the faintest to the most intense, in which the gravitation of the outside worlds overwhelms the man-senses and absorbs the inner unit. *In fact, the lightest and faintest form of dream is the very thoughts that we think.* The dream-state deepening, through its shades, as it were, of colour; or sinking, through its *diapason* or register of sounds, until it thickens, in the former case (as it may be said) into the darkest of withdrawal out of this life, or into trance, or ecstasy. Or grows the more ponderous, severe and sonorous, in the latter instance (to liken it to another strange, universal —*sense*—music:)—as it degenerates *downwards* into bass. We always dream in life. And the guage is according to the amount of absorption out of this world. Or the undulating, and returning to the world, flights, which the intelligence takes into the worlds not about us.

The highest step in the system of visions is ecstasy—a removal from the world of the senses, so that the subject of the visions remains in a purely internal world, mostly without external participation.

A certain natural disposition is necessary to the higher state of ecstasy; but it may be produced by outward and artificial means. The gases and vapours by which the priests of old become ecstatic, or which were used upon the oracles, may be classed among the narcotics. The most violent convulsions were connected with somnambulism, as in the case of the priestess of Apollo, at Delphi. Incense, and the bewildering dances of the Turkish dervishes, also produce dizziness and prophetic visions, similar to those observed in the priests of antiquity—in the Sabaism of the Canaanites, in the service of Baal, in the Indian Schiwa and Kali, in the Phœnician Moloch, in the Bacchanalian festivals of the Greeks and Romans, and, at the present day, among the Lapps and Finns.

Persons of great imagination, with an excitable nervous system and of impressible temperament, and particularly those of a religious turn of mind, are especially inclined to natural ecstasy. Poets and artists, as well as enthusiasts who are sunk in religious contemplations, are often thrown into an ecstatic state by very slight causes. Those ideas which float so constantly around them form their world of the spirit; and, on the contrary, the real world is, to them, but a field on which the invisible ideas are reflected, or they carry its impressions, with them, to the realms of the mind. Poets and artists, therefore, often possess, in common with those persons who are naturally inclined to abnormal convulsions, an easily-excited temperament. "For in the inner recesses of the mind," says Cicero, "is divine prophecy hidden and confined, as the soul, without reference to the body, may be moved by a divine impulse." "Without this," Democritus maintains, "there can be no poet," in which Plato also agrees. It was thus that the painter Angelico da Fiesole often fell into ecstatic states while painting, and had in them ideal visions. Michael Angelo says of a picture painted by him, that "No man could have created such a picture without having seen the original." (Görres' Mystic, I., 155.)

In the senses we are as the telescope, in the perfect sight-making of the optic glasses. Man is in the *focus* of his glasses of senses. But there are other landscapes than that made to him. And new sights float over, and through, the man-perspectives, and, in new adjustments of the preter-natural soul-sight, new worlds are penetrated to, or (which is the same) undulate, centrically, to us, from out the universal flat of shows. For nothing was ever destroyed, neither is there anything new. Time, or things ;—by which we mean, We ;—fade out of things. The belief of a thing, being all of it. This is pure Berkeleyan Immaterialism, and it was believed in by the ancient philosophers, and suspected by the commentators and examiners of them, of the middle ages. Basis of the Rosicrucian secret system, and of all mysticism or occult knowledge, it is the only thing *possible*, granting that other things are possible.

Anything very unexpected, new, or striking snatches us, instantly, out of this world. And we experience that which we call *a shock*. We can glow, by working, as by heavy strokes upon our nature, as like iron in the forge. And this, with an exalting light, forced out—the Immortal fire-wealth—out of another world, even to grow visible to men's mortal eyes. This is possession, ecstasy, and the Divine Illumination. None the less real, because we see nothing of it in the world. Else we should be—as the Bible says—Gods.

It is in this magical world of God's light, that Sainthood becomes possible, and that the solid world and the exterior nature obey the Godlike nature, like machinery:—worked and drawn, magically, into the circle of its power, as by the all-compelling magnetism. Trodden of the Spirit!

Children's life is dream-life. It is a God-instinctive, magic life, in which unliving things are, really, taken to live. Children's life is another and a different thing to our life. And children, to a certain extent, exercise an enchanted invigoration—or a preternatural and extra-sense of which we know nothing. But which the thinker can suspect. This is the origin, and the meaning, of the sacrifice of children, in some secret, unhallowed rites.

Thus much we urge to show that the thing, Dream, is as an alphabet; man passing through *that meant* by all the letters, from the simple *alpha*, or the ordinary man's thought, downwards through all the middle or lower letters. And that, doubtless, the quicker, and the more perfectly, as his powers are the greater, and of the intenser character. And—even in this world—as sinking out of this world, until he subsides, past his magic and preternatural Sleep (rightly considered), in which all the worlds open, or, rather, in which the divested soul sees cleared of the world's day-delusions which man calls his truths. And all which the soul wears, in its senses, as a thinner or thicker *garment of circumstances.* Thus it falls—this soul—past all the *strata,* or bands of its supernatural possibilities, even in this life, until it engulphs in the last slumber of all—namely, death. And which is, moreover, in the truth, a gate, of day-light, out of darkness; a new birth out of old death. In short, that death is life, in place of death, and life is death. A life of death which, notwithstanding, in this death of life, our body —the machine—cries out against, in every atom, as the, in every way, to be run from and shunned!

Thus is mortal and immortal reverse of each other. Man, in this life, wanting no other life.

The mysterious meaning of baptism by water is a symbolism prevailing through all faiths, Heathen and Christian. It is that of the earliest traditional or the Pythagorean transmigration, not adjudged as by its vulgar reading, but as signifying the *onward dissolution,* into nothingness, of being, that is, of this being, through the farthest separated (save air, in which man always is, and therefore always is baptised) matter:—water! This, therefore, is the only element for a rite. Holy water, and ablution, also signify the same. Thence, as from that next-loosest of matter—water, the only possible symbol for a rite, Man is delivered into the farther, supernatural, airy changes, where matter ceases—loosening utterly from about him. And, then, the spirit or the fire, begins, taking up the matter-undulations. This is the freedom into the foundation, or inspiring, Light;—the Nirvâna of the Buddhists;—the God Flame of the Magi;—the Holy Spirit of the Christians;—the everything, out of this state, and the nothing in it, of all religions. Life—nay, all existence—being considered as a Purgatory of a severer or a more assuasive order. And, therefore, being evil—or God's Shadow—for the very reason of its being Life—or consciousness at all. All consciousness being defect—all the outside world being evil.

The above is the mystic meaning of that text in the Holy Testament where St. John is described as declaring:—" I indeed baptise you with water unto repentance : but he that comes after me is mightier than I, whose shoes I am not worthy to bear : he shall baptise you with the Holy Ghost, AND WITH FIRE." St Matthew, chapter 3, verse 11.

" In one way or another, everybody has been, once, powerfully stimulated to inquire into the grand mystery of his existence, and his relations to the un-seen world." And men's higher powers are not of this world. Genius, while it is in its fit, really does loosen the worlds about us. As to the sleeper, real things, quite out of this world, are shown through the symbolical, and often absurd, machinery of dreams; so lights of truth—and the *truth of truth*—glance to us through the distorting and impossible fogs of the mythologies.

Reproach us not with stimulating a new uneasiness in man. Ask us not the use of the mysticism into which we declare man's eternal interests transcend. Charge us not with making trouble out of that so commonplace as change—decay—disappearance out of this pleasant world of ours. Confound us not with these real things which you have in your hands. Fall not back so confidently, and so triumphantly, upon this world which you think you have so surely to yourself. So surely, as you think you have this world! as that, in those secret thoughts which you tell to no one, you can make—and that with the best feelings and through the mere infirmity of nature—the disappearance of other men out of the world as a sort of sad pastime to you. As a means of private consolation that you, at least, are still in it. Trample not down our preaching, with so much certainty—O men of the world!—with that matter of fact of yours. Let us see, indeed, whether you have this world so safely within your grasp as you suppose.

Now, do we not all, sometimes, feel, in that intense self-persuasion which, somehow, seems to admit us sometimes behind the scenes of this play of the world, that all the visible, and all that we have dreamt, beheld, suffered—nay, known of it, is but our own opinion? Have you not, yourself, our thoughtful reader, at some by-time or rare time, been stopped in your many-folded meditation, and then been made to see, as in the flash of an instant, and as all out of yourself, as it were, that your whole life of days has been the mere dream dreamt? Have you not, at one time or other, seemed, in a single moment's exaltation, to "see through it all," as the phrase expresses it? Have you not beheld your whole life as a picture in the mirror of your own mind, which represented the mind, but nothing out of it? Have you not—and do not be so hasty in your denial, because it seems so strange that it should be so—in a moment's dispossession out of yourself, caught the apparently impossible glimpse into truth, exposing the whole fabric of things but as the mere appearance to you as yourself? As the Appearance conjured but in the hollow of your own brain? This is the whole secret, and intent, and meaning of the immaterial philosophy of Berkeley—of the views of Plato—of the magic reveries of the Buddhists.

Now, without the Immediate Spirit of God, it is universal cloudland. Without the Divine Possession it is we—as men—that make this or that;—that manufacture the materials of the world. There is nothing of man really out of ourselves. The world of human-reason is no more than the relation between man and the world, supplying the means of seeing that world, which means are it. Therefore is the devil Lucifer, or the Lord of the Light of the World, or of Human Reason! Human Reason being as dead ashes in the attainment to the idea of God!

There is no such thing as the ordinary sense in the great, general sense. The several senses are only particular arcs of the great circle of sense. Our nature denies us the possibility of seeing the whole at once.

The moments in which we feel that wheel of sense are our sight, our hearing, our touch, and those other instants of perception that we label as our senses. But apart from time (the grand microscope), in which alone we are made to feel it, it is the whole circle that is revolving, as it is but the whole sense that, in any particular sense, we—as it were—place the momentary finger upon. Time is but man's instant of it. We are the measure, but not that we measure.

> " All else is cut away before,
> And closes from behind."

Now, with the lights of the exquisite sense, we gain, in philosophy, only the non-entity in which we lose ourselves. Infallibly, in learning, we arrive at that tremendous precipice of unbelief over which— over the very brink of which—as in the face of our very fears, we are urged to look on clouds. In all human acquirement, as in our dark island of mortality, in dumb despair round we appeal! Do we not know that in our learning, and in our penetration, using the wings of the human reason, ALONE, as the sails to urge us as into this void exterior of the world, the whole machinery can be melted as into philosophic NOTHING, and that the very great glory, which is as the life of all, can be even extended and prolonged—light of light, as all of the conceivable—until it SHINE a BLANK? *A blank of perfection in which glory, itself, shall grow but purposeless, and therefore nothing!*

Therefore may we pray the great God who filleth all space, and who is not only space, but is even our thought of it, to assist us, with our man's thoughts alone, never to rise. For in that great desert of the mind where there are no facts and no possibilities, without the unreasoning, all-believing, God-lighted ignorance of childhood itself (which is wholly filled with miracle), there is the certainty of expiring extenuate. Man's true saving, in his knowledge, is the being baffled, and in the sinking. That, in sinking from those presumptuous metaphysic cloud-heights, he may, in his very fall strike the happy foot again upon those steps of common-sense! Those stairs of knowledge up which, as the climbing of the Tower of Babel, he mounted. Even strike ground again; with the anchors of the world, that man may find his God!

And it is some such thoughts as these that drew men into the deserts; converted workers and toilers, in the world, into visionaries. The insufficiency of the world induced the thinker to look about for other solacements. The sense of the swiftness of time, and the persuasion that not a day was to be lost if regard was to be paid to his future concerns, instigated many a devotee to seek another and immortal kingdom that should dawn to him amidst the cloister. If men were adequately impressed with the wonders of nature— with the mysteries that surround them—with the capacities that are born in them—with the story of the generations, and with the unfruitful prospect, to the dwellers in this state, of the wearying, on-coming, self-repeating centuries :—new years of suns, countless revolutions of moons :—if such were, but for a moment, the upward sight, how would men rest in the mean turmoil, application to which makes the business of life from the cradle—even to that dreadful moment in which we are surprised in it!

CHAPTER XV.

DREAMS AND THE DREAM-STATE.

WHAT are dreams? No one has, as yet, thought well about them.

Since there is no correspondence between the sense of the one world and that of the other.

Yet, if, as we have sought to demonstrate, this world in which we, living men, exist is only made sense in the conditions of the waking being; is, in fact, a thing accepted, but not absolutely true; then the world of sleep may be a TRUE WORLD, whose life is only distorted, like the images through the wrong telescope, which are only untrue as coming to "us" in our own non-corresponding medium. The very fact of "sleep"—rightly looked at—proves the world, in this sense, only an accident.

We are as the telescope. The wrong sight, in which the false and monstrous images go flying, requires to be reduced into the correct perspectives:— into the corresponding (that is, corresponding to us; otherwise to our senses) adjustment of the glasses when we gain a *focus*, and, to our delight—a microcosm, a world opens!

Swimming skies, tree and cloud—these, solid and as blocks—mountains like men, and men like mountains; animate objects dead, and inanimate objects breathing, living, speaking:—absurd *sentences of action*, because the words have no judgment-stops between, Time being struck out of the story of dreams, and the things alone remaining without Time to play them in :—All the madness, overrolling and contending, in fact, of the confused, telescopic field; how soon is all this reduced into order (as even into the proper, recognisable real world) when we have seized the right sight-point; as, in other words, when we have gone deep enough down in our dreams for the glasses —as the new faculty, or the new magic—to give us this other world. This dream world.

God has reserved sleep for his own world. Therein as time is annihilated, remain centuries in which shall the spirit act. Therein are lives—histories of the past—back into which the sleeper, freed from his chains of flesh, is nightly carried. There all the great worlds open. And the very incoherency of dreams— their very seeming madness—arises only from the fact of Time and Space being struck out from them. When we awake, both these return, and the dream is absurd. The bridge is broken down behind us, over which we have come, out of sleep, back into our waking world! And that life of dreams—if we recall it at all—is a mad life, into which no consent of ours is asked if we should again go. Disburthening our-selves of our sense-judgment when we enter into it. And why are dreams the wild children of an Impos-sible Realm?

Because measures shall have that they measure. Because senses shall have that to make them. Be-cause the field of arithmetic shall have its figures. And our measures are of a world. Our senses are of flesh. Our figures are of a region of marks. We are *in* the dreams:—strangers in a strange land. The dreams are not in us; else should we constitute *them*, making the dominant sense *our* sense. An author—wonderful in his suggestive writing—the brilliant, super-sensual truth of whose composition hath been gained by his projected genius — under, perhaps, opium-inspiration—being sped through the imagination-lighted depths of his own fervid and grand mind; stumbling on immortal shadowy jewels:—this profound thinker has said:—

"In the English rite of 'Confirmation,' by personal choice, and by sacramental oath, each man says, in effect—'Lo! I rebaptise myself. And that which, once, was sworn on my behalf, now I swear for myself.' Even so, in dreams, perhaps, under some secret conflict of the midnight sleeper, lighted up to consciousness at the time, but darkened to the memory as soon as all is finished, even each several child of our mysterious race may complete, for himself, the aboriginal fall."

Is not this singular passage mysteriously suggestive?

May we not undervalue dreams?

May we understand anything concerning their true nature?

CHAPTER XVI.

MAGNETIC SPECULATIONS.

MAN may be esteemed as the medium, means, or channel through which (by his vital, sensitive, magnetic centrically self-forcing, or the intensely thinking operation) are drawn in and agitated the circumambient spiritual *media*—more or less instinct with the possibility of life and the palpability of life.

The human being projects these in circumvolving, spiritual, outward, unconscious enforcements; which are as the sensitive undulation of the Inner Life, flowing free through the material, as that with which it hath nought of common. It may be said to touch and break upon another similar super-sensual, magnetic wave; propelled, perhaps, in like manner, from re-motest personal distance, and proceeding from another individuality, incorporate or not.

This may be prefiguration; as rolling through a neighbouring outer ring of life, *not yet* subsided, or darkened into *human* sense. It may be as a centri-fugatory, magnetic disturbance, or as a " rising again into the palpable," of a past vital ring; whole, part, or concrete; according to the power of this unsus-pected life-magic, so, from his centre, exerted by the human breather.

In these concinctures, or rings of extra-vital, un-imaginable soul-capacity—whose laws must be unknown to us—may lie spiritual disclosures; apparitions; the whole range of the supernatural, whether palpable supernaturalism, or supernatural shadows. For the former, indeed, is possible.

Here may lie all that assumes the form of the hypernatural. For we err in accepting this world— as we have repeated often—as, philosophically, a real thing. It is " as a microcosm," suddenly struck to view out of the instantaneous happy adjustment of the object-glasses; as of the telescope. The telescope, which may be taken as *ourselves in our true man's sensual and perfect corporeal state.* This it is which makes that choice panorama which is the sum of our true mathematical, right lined senses. These cannot be philosophically conceived as existing out of us.

For the truest of this world, is possibly the falsest of another. Therefore supernatural prefiguration, or anticipative magical disclosures—as they seem— whether " read" or " unread" (by which we mean recognised or not) :—of which there stand, in the candid and unprejudiced thinker's mind, undoubted *common-sense* record :—these may lie *forward* in the circumvolving future multiform regions of being. As it were; *blinks*—so to speak—in the hypersensual cloud, or medium—knots in the texture, thwart-working in the precipitated world-scheme, cross-produced sparks of light as in the backward flowing waves of the great sea.

But all this may be quite short of that ultimate objectless, extenuate world which contains all things (the *Nirvâna* of the Buddhists again), and into which all motion whatever, as all life and being, are melted. For man's theological and (nowhere authorised), limitation of simply *this life* and *another life,* in the Things to Be, is manifestly—to the thinker—as narrow and insufficient a conclusion as it is unsatisfactory and childlike. And this without the grand instinctive Revelation which is in the minds of children.

In magnetism lies the key to unlock the future science of magic, to fertilise the growing germs in cultivated fields of knowledge, and reveal the wonders of the creative mind.

True magic lies in the most secret and inmost powers of the mind. Our spiritual nature is still, as it were, barred within us. All spiritual wonders, in the end, become but wonders of our minds.

Magic is a great, secret, sudden, and disbelieved-in, wisdom (out of this world, and its opposite). Reason is a great, public, relied-on mistake (in this world), and the same with it, in its, by-man, accepted operations. The one leads down, and destroys the world. The other springs with it, and makes it. Therefore is one the worldlily true and believed, since man makes himself in it, and grows, into his being, in it. And therefore is the other, in the world-judgment, false and a lie, and a juggle, since man is contradicted in it. So says Paracelsus.

"The existence of a universal medium was suspected by the ancients. It was the φύσις of Hippocrates, Aristotle, and Galen ; the *anima* (as opposed to *animus*), of the Romans : and the Sephiroth of the Jewish Cabbala. From this 'soul of the world' of the pre-Platonic Orientals all souls are emanations. The 'demons' of the Greeks, from Plato down to Iamblichus, were nothing but this. By this the magicians of the Nile, and the jugglers of the Ganges, wrought their wonders. This was the true Python, source of all divination, magic, and witchcraft, in annals sacred and profane. This was the true Secret of the Protean wonders of rhabdomancy, clairvoyance, and animal magnetism."

Thus writes a modern author. He further says that:—"What the ancients suspected, the moderns have demonstrated. In every chemic, or vital function of the body, with electricity, another imponderable, diverse from electricity, is evolved. Three independent courses of experiment, by Matteucci, Thilorier and Lafontaine, and Reichenbach, coincided with the report of Arago on Angelique Cottin, in establishing the discovery. Transmissible through electric non-conductors, capable of accumulation in non-isolated bodies, possessing polarity, residing in the magnet with, but distinct from, magnetism, visible in darkness to sensitive organs, energising from the organism upon nature, and reacting, from nature, upon the organism, it pervades the earth and heavenly bodies, is diffused through space, and is the agent of the phenomena of Clairvoyance.

"Instrumental representative of mind, the brain is capable of spontaneous action, without mind. Such spontaneous action will be indistinguishable from mental operations proper. Moreover, as the human countenance photographs itself upon the sensitive silverplate which it does not touch, so the human brain may odylise itself upon the sensitive cerebral plate of the medium which it does not touch. Or, as in every cranium two brains unite to form a double cerebral unit, so, in space, two brains, filmily meshed together by odylic threads, may virtually unite to form a double cerebral unit, the impressions of the stronger imparting themselves to and through the weaker. Thus things never known to the medium, apparently, or to any one in a magnetic circle, may be given forth by the distant automatic agency of some co-efficient brain.

" That such communications should affirm themselves to be of spiritual origin, is no more wonderful than the fictitious personality affirmed by the insane, the hypochondriac, or even the dreaming brain. Under pathematic treatment, the impressible subject becomes whatever the operator pleases, male or female, human, divine, or infernal. So by the operation of drugs and philtres, as in the case of Madame Ranfaing, all the phenomena of the demoniac possession have been permanently established.

" Now, suppose that the brain of the medium be in odylic *rapport* with the brain of some inmate of a lunatic asylum, or of some visionary enthusiast or monomaniac, and thus to appearance only, and, of course, falsely receive communications from Benjamin Franklin, Thomas Paine, or any other remarkable individual. Or assume that it may be *en rapport* with some brain dreaming, or drugged, or pathetised, or hallucinated, or intoxicated, or even highly poetic and enthusiastic, or nervous, and thus receive the impress of a counterfeit personality.

" Thus any highly-wrought cerebral excitement might be supposed to telegraph itself, across the globe, upon any other brain in due odylic *rapport*, and communicate intelligence of then passing events.

" As to events so far in the past that they cannot exist in the form of impressions on any living brain, it is only necessary to conceive that they have recorded themselves eternally upon the all-pervading odylic medium. They may leave their impress, not recognisable indeed by sense, but real. The brain of the medium, or its odylic co-efficient, or other half, comes into such a susceptible state that all these phantoms, held in odylic suspense, as it were, type themselves thereon, and are given forth, as before explained, in automatic discharge.

" And even future events, in some such way, might be supposed of being capable of being *sensed* by the brain."

That extended, encircling twilight-world which everywhere would seem as the *penumbra* of the full light, and of the central sun of the healthy human mind (in which other things than real things are dimmed), has been, by philosophers, faintly caught an idea of, as not only the conqueror of the possibility of chance to man (as containing everything to happen to him), but also as a dawn in which everything is, but only not yet arrived at. The future lifting from off us as the darkness of the night, and leaving no objects.

CHAPTER XVII.

THEOSOPHISTS AND FIRE-PHILOSOPHERS.

THE Fire-Philosophers, or *Philosophi per ignem*, were a fanatical sect of philosophers who appeared towards the close of the sixteenth century. They made a figure in almost all the countries of Europe. They declared that the intimate essences of natural things were only to be known by the trying effects of fire, directed in a chemical process. The Theosophists, also, insisted that human reason was a dangerous and deceitful guide; that no real progress could be made in knowledge, or in religion, by it, and that to all vital, that is, supernatural purpose, it was a vain thing. They taught that divine and supernatural exaltation was the only means of arriving at truth. Their name of Paracelsists was derived from Paracelsus, the eminent physician and chemist, who was the chief ornament of this extraordinary sect. In England, Robert Flood, or Fludd, was their great advocate and exponent. Rivier, who wrote in France; Severinus, an author of Denmark; Kunrath, an eminent physician of Dresden; and Daniel Hoffmann, professor of divinity in the University of Helmstadt, have also treated largely on Paracelsus, and on his system.

Philippus Aureolus Theophrastus Paracelsus was born, in 1493, at Einsielden, a small town of the canton of Schwitz, distant some leagues from Zurich.

Having passed a troubled, migratory, and changeful life, this great chemist, and very original thinker, died on the 24th of September, 1541, in the Hospital of St. Stephen, in the 48th year of his age. His works may be ennumerated as follow. 1. German editions Basil. 1575, in 8vo. Ib. i. 1589-90: in 10 vols., 4to; and Strasbourg, 1603-18, in 4 vols., folio 2. The Latin editions. *Opera omnia Medico-chymico-chirugica,* Francfurt, 1603, in 10 vols., 4to; and Geneva, 1658, in 3 vols., fol. 3. The French editions. *La Grande Chirurgie de Paracelse,* Lyons, 1593, and 1603, in 4to, and Montbeliard, 1608, in 8vo. See Adelung. *Histoire de la Folie Humaine :* tom. vii. *Biographie Universelle,* article *Paracelse ;* and Sprengel, *Histoire pragmatique de la Medecine,* tom. iii.

"Akin to the school of the ancient Fire-Believers, and of the Magnetists of a later period," says the learned Dr. Ennemoser, in his History of Magic (most ably rendered into English by William Howitt): —" of the same cast as these speculators and searchers into the mysteries of nature, drawing from the same well, are the Theosophists of the sixteenth and seventeenth centuries. These practised chemistry, by which they asserted that they could explain the profoundest secrets of nature. As they strove, above all earthly knowledge, after the divine, and sought the divine light and fire, through which all men can acquire the true wisdom, they were called the Fire-Philosophers (*Philosophi per ignem*). The most distinguished of these are Theophrastus Paracelsus, Adam Von Boden, Oswald Croll; and, later, Valentine Weigel, Robert Flood or Fludd, Jacob

Böhmen, Peter Poiret, &c." Under this head, we may also refer to the Medico-surgical Essays of Hermann, published at Berlin in 1778; and Pfaff's Astrology.

As a great general principle, the Theosophists called the soul a fire, taken from the eternal ocean of light.

In regard of the supernatural—using the word in its widest sense—it may be said that "all the difficulty in admitting the strange things told us, lies in the non-admission of an internal causal world *as absolutely* real : it is said, in *intellectually* admitting, because the influence of the arts proves that men's feelings always have admitted, and do still admit, this reality."

The Platonic philosophy of vision is that it is the view of objects really existing in interior light, which assume form, not according to arbitrary laws, but according to the state of mind. This interior light, if we understand Plato, unites with exterior light in the eye, and is thus drawn into a sensual or imaginative activity; but when the outward light is separated, it reposes in its own serene atmosphere.

From any given point, in height, that the intellect is able to achieve, the SAME SPIRIT downward SYNTHESISES into Manifestation;—upwards DISSIPATES into God!

In other words, before any knowledge of God can be formed at all, IT MUST HAVE A SHAPE.

CHAPTER XVIII.

THE TEMPLARS AND THE FIRE-PHILOSOPHY.

THERE is little doubt that the great men, and in-quiring spirits, among the Templars had penetrated to this revelation of the ever-living, supernatural fire, or had been taught it (as a treasured truth) by the Saracens. And it is supposable that, at the suppression of this grand, warlike, and monastic order—so bound by the injunctions of a secret *formula*, which, in all the persecutions of the Camps or Lodges, never appeared to the eyes of the world, but was denied;—many of the things of which they were accused, such as magical ceremonies and Pagan rites, wizard-trances and sacrifices, outrages of the Cross and so forth, were satisfactorily established (in their trials), as matters of which they were indisputably guilty. It is impossible to believe but that there was something more in the denouncement and extinction, at the same time, all over Europe, of those religio-knightly or monastic-military orders—in whose ranks fought, and taught, some men of the most powerful, and most daring, understanding of the period—than the jealousy of their power, and the desire of their riches and worldly accumulation. That secret and forbidden studies were pursued by them; that under the protection and yet in the refusal (as it were) of the Cross, and as from behind their holy and militarily wondrous character, the arch-leaders among them (whether chieftains of mind or of arms) closely hung on the track of philosophy until it evanished into transcendentalism, or the supposed atheistic, and by occult and cabalistic means established relations with the unseen, seeking to traffic with the spiritual world, is very likely.

The round form of their " temples"—as they were styled by the brotherhood;—their various *insignia* and habits;—their secret Book;—their rites—all seem to bespeak a knowledge of the heathen fire-idolatry :—misunderstood and perverted, in the hands of all but those, who, of the order, had risen to the highest knowledge in it—and who rose to *Truth*— into the indulgence of sensual appetites and the denial of the future life, and, consequently, of the fullest and the morally darkest, though the most worldlily luscious epicureanism.

Whilst, perhaps, the chiefs of the Order of the Templars had penetrated to truths the most astonishing, though, necessarily, undivulgeable (especially in that superstitious and ignorant age; of which, incontestably, they were far forward), they paid the usual penalty of their great knowledge in being decried and burnt as magicians. Simply because the time was not prepared—if, indeed, any time should be—for that which they could tell. They, and their whole body, therefore, appeared, in the exaggerations of the Church, and in the magnifying medium of the terror which their doings inspired, as thirsting for impossible things. Climbing, as in their cowls and mail, as by a storming ladder of presumptuously supposed lightning-proof, steel, and under the mask and shield of the Cross, into the imagined, accursed chambers of the magic, devilish Fire: the treasure-house, or home, or Hell of the forbidden gods, rich in all possible ethereal and human splendours!

The famous Beauséant,* or banner of the Templars, was parti-coloured :—that is, divided down the centre, in two halves of "black and white." This figuring-forth of the utterly opposed colours, is generally taken to signify the immitigable hatred of the Templars for the Infidels, but their abiding love and benignity towards the Christians. This total friendship, or uncompromising abnegation would be heraldically denoted in the perfect contrast of the black and white halves, or "fields," of the Templars' ensign, divided *parti-per-pale*. But, when we remember that the Egyptians mythed their Perfect Divinity, or Cause of All, under (of this world) the hopeless, empty colour *Black*, in opposition to White, or Matter-Light which was taken to signify "This World, and the Glory of this World;" and, when we recall that the proper robes, or vestments, of magicians, when invested in their cabalistic panoply and armed for charms—as directed by the authentic formula—are of the colours white and black, we grow into another sort of belief regarding the meaning of this Templar banner, mystic and heathenish as it is, and we conclude that it fell back, for its real hieroglyph, upon the Fire-Creed. This faith of the fierce deistical East, and of the Guebre, Gubh, or Gaur. And this, surely, not without reason.

---

* The flags of Prussia are white, with a deep black upper and lower border. This is derived from the banner of the Templars, which again repeats the mystic black and white of the Egyptians.

Nor does the Order of the Knights of St. John of Jerusalem, who, in the grandeur of their stately galleys, made of the Mediterranean a royal sea, and elevated the Islands of Malta, and of Rhodes, almost into the splendours of an empire set on the water; nor does this order escape the imputation of wrong-doing:—of being betrayed in the signs and the hieroglyphs of the secret, reprobated, Infidel doctrine. Their colours, the fashion of their arms, and their attire, in which—in priestly or any other orders or communities—lies much of meaning, glance-up to justifiable Christian suspicion in the wizard, heretical half-light. In short, we hold the Teutonic Knights, or the soldier monks of St. John of Jerusalem, as equally as the Templars, as very questionable Christians. Though this imagined infidelity might be only confined to the Heads of the Chapters: the great body of the Knights being merely directed.

In the prosecutions of the Knights Templars, which are generally known, a certain mystification and secrecy may be observed; as if the whole of the charges against them were not brought publicly out. This arose from various causes. The persecuted were really very religious, and were bound by the most solemn Masonic oaths (and Masonry was intimately connected with these matters) not to divulge the secrets of the order. The impression is very general that these persecutions were undertaken for the sake of the wealth of the order. This, we think, is a mistake. There were other, and deeper—and necessary —reasons.

The strange and heathenish doctrines to which

allusion has before been made, are visible everywhere in the curious mystical figures always seen upon the monuments of the Templars; in the fishes, bound together by the tails, on the tombs of Italy, and appearing on the vaulting of the Temple Church, London; — in the astrological emblems on many churches, such as the Zodiacs on the floor of the Church of St. Irenæus at Lyons, and on a church at York, and Notre Dame at Paris, and Bacchus, or the God I.H.S., filling the wine-cask, formerly on the floor of the Church of St. Denis. Again, in the round Churches of the Templars, in imitation of the round church at Jerusalem, probably built by them in the Circlar, or Cyclar, or Gilgal form, in allusion to various recondite subjects, and in the monograms I H Σ and X H in thousands of places.

At every turn we meet with some remnant of Paganism. It is a very extraordinary thing that the Christian Templars should call themselves Templars in honour of the Temple, the destruction of which all Christians boasted of as a miraculous example of Divine wrath in their favour to Christians. This goes to prove the Templars much older than the Crusades, and that the pretended origin of these people is totally false. There is a certain suspicion entertained, not without reason, that the origin of this community may be looked for in the College of Cashi, and the Temple of Solomon in Cashmere, or the lake, or mere, of Cashi. The Gymnosophists, the Kasideans, the Essenes, the Therapeutæ, the Dionesians, the Eleusinians, the Pythagoreans, the Chaldeans were, in reality, all an order of religionists, including among them, and consisting in great part of, an order of Monks, who were, in fact, the heads of the society.

The Teutonic Knights seem to have been the first instituted. But it is thought that they were grafted upon a class of persons—charitable devotees—who had settled themselves, as the historians say, near the Temple at Jerusalem, to assist poor Christian pilgrims who visited it; although the real temple had disappeared even to the last stone, for a thousand years. This shows how little use these historians make of their understandings. The Teutonic Knights are said to have come from Germany, from the Teutonic tribes. Let us hasten to relieve North Germany from the weighty and undeserved honour. The word Teut is Tat, and Tat is Buddha. The name of Buddha, with some of the German nations, was Tuisto or Tuisco, derived from whose name comes our day of the week—Tuesday. From Tuisto or Tuisco came the Teutones, *Teutisci*, and the Teutonic Knights, and the name of Mercury Teuisco. Perhaps, Mercury *Tris*megistus.

The round church of Jerusalem, built by Helena, the mystic Helena (daughter of Coilus), mother of Constantine, who was born at York, and the chapter-houses at York, and at other cathedrals, were reproductions of the circular Stonehenge and Abury. The choirs of many of the cathedrals in France and England are built crooked of the nave of the church, for the same reason, whatever that might be, that the Druidical temple is so built at Classerniss in Scotland. All the round *chapter-houses* of our Cathedrals were built round for the same reason that the Churches of the Templars were round.   In these chapters and the crypts, till the thirteenth century, the secret religion was celebrated far away from the profane vulgar. These buildings have been thought to be the representative successors of the caves of India, and afterwards of the cupola-formed buildings there, of the Cyclopean Treasury of Atreus at Mycenæ, and of the Labyrinths of which we read in Egypt, Crete, Italy, &c.   These labyrinths could be only for the purposes of religion, and, it is not to be doubted, of that religion of the Cyclopes which universally prevailed. The underground crypts of our cathedrals, with their forests of pillars, were labyrinths in miniature.   There is something about the circular churches of the Templars which seems very remarkable.   We have only four in England, we believe, of the churches of the Templars :—namely, those in London, at Maplestead in Essex, at Northampton, and at Cambridge; —and they are all round.   This form, we are told, was adopted in imitation of the round church at Jerusalem.   But how came the church at Jerusalem to be round?   And how came these Christian Knights to be called by the name of the detested Jewish Temple ?

The Templars were divided into orders exactly after the system of the Assassins.   Knights, Esquires, and Lay-Brethren answered to the Refeck, Fedavee, and Lascek of the Assassins; as the Prior, Grand-Prior, and Grand-Master of the former correspond with the Dai, Dai-al-Kebir, and Sheik of the mountain of the latter.

As the Ishmaelite Refeck was *clad in white*, with

I.

a *red mark of distinction*, so the Knight of the Temple wore a white mantle, adorned with a red mark of distinction—the red cross. It is remarkable that they were called "Illuminators." And it is to be suspected that the *red* mark of distinction, kept back as common to both Templars and Ishmaelites, was a red eight-point cross, or a *red rose* on a *cross*.

In the fourth number of the "Foreign Quarterly Review," Art. II., p. 464, may be found a very interesting account of the Templars. But it is scarcely a correct one. For upon the innocence of the Templars of Gnosticism, there are various matters, in their history, totally unaccountable. There is scarcely a word, however, of the crimes, to the extent charged, to be believed against them. The greater number of them were, doubtless, innocent and ignorant enough. But various suspicions occur in the instance of the mysterious symbol of the "Red-Cross Knights." Their badge, the red cross with *eight points*, is the monogram of the Buddhists of Tibet, and of the Manichæans. This badge was a real Talisman. Concerning this important identity, see "Asiatic Researches," vol. x. In peace, this symbol commanded the rights of hospitality. In war—though fighting on opposite sides—one "red cross" would not, individually, strike another.

The Templars were accused of worshipping a being called Bahúmid and Bafomet, or Kharuf. Von Hammer says that this word, written in Arabic, has the meaning of "Calf," and is what Kircher calls *Anima Mundi*. It is difficult not to believe that this "Kharuf" is our "Calf." The Assassins are said to have worshipped a Calf. If these latter have a Calf in use as an emblem, it may be justly considered as a proof that, contrary to the prevailing ideas concerning them, they are a tribe of extreme antiquity; which, though holding the doctrines of the Ten Incarnations, yet still clings to the ancient worship of Taurus. There is a picture, in Russia, of the Holy Family, in which the Calf is found instead of the Ram. A learned author pronounces that the doctrines of the Assassins and the Templars were the same.

All Temples were surrounded with pillars recording the numbers of the constellations, the signs of the Zodiac, or the cycles of the planets; and each *Templum* was supposed, in some way, to be a microcosm, or symbol, of the Temple of the universe, or of the starry vault called *Templum*. It was this Templum of the universe from which the Knights Templars took their name, and not from the individual Temple at Jerusalem, built probably by their predecessors, and destroyed many years before the time allotted for their rise; but which rise, it is suspected, was only a revivification from a state of depression into which they had fallen.

All the Temples were imitative—were microcosms of the celestial *Templum*—and on this account they were surrounded with pillars recording astronomical subjects, and intending both to do honour to these subjects and to keep them in perpetual remembrance. We have records of every cycle except of that of the Beast, 666. We have, in Abury, the cycles of 650—608—600—60—40—30—19—12, &c. We have the *forty* pillars around the Temple of Chilminar in

Persia; the Temple at Baalbec with forty pillars; the Tucte-Solomon, on the frontiers of China, in Tartary, called also the Temple of the *forty pillars*. There is the same number in each, and probably for the same reason. Forty is one of the most common numbers in the Druidical Temples. In the Temples at Pæstum, on each side of the Temple, fourteen pillars record the Egyptian cycle of the *dark and light** sides of the moon as described by Plutarch; and the whole thirty-eight which surround them record the two Metonic cycles, so often found in the Druidical Temples. All Temples were originally open at the top; so that twelve pillars curiously described the belt of the Zodiac, and the vault of heaven the roof.

Theatres were originally Temples, where the *mythos* was scenically represented. And until they were abused they were intended for nothing else. But it is evident that, for this purpose, a peculiar construction of the Temple was necessary. When Scaurus built a Theatre in Greece, he surrounded it with 360 pillars. The Temple at Mecca was surrounded with 360 stones. And, in like manner, with the same number the Templum at Iona, in Scotland, was surrounded. The Templars were nothing but one branch of Masons, perhaps a branch to which the care of some peculiar part of Temples was entrusted; and there is probability that the name of Templars was only another name for Casideans.

In the Western part of Asia, in the beginning of

---

* The reader will remember what we have already stated regarding the magic banner of the Templars, Beauséant, and the Prussian colours.

the twelth century, the sect or religious tribe called Ishmaelians, or Battenians, or Assassins, arose. These "Assassins" were first noticed, in the Western world, with their chief Hakem Bemrillah, or Hakem-biamr-allah, who was held up, in Syria, as the Tenth Avatar, or, as it is assumed, incarnation. His ideas of God were very refined. The first of the creatures of God, the only production *immediate* of his power, was the *intelligence universelle*, which showed itself at each of the manifestations of the Divinity on earth; that by means of this minister, all creatures were made, and he was the Mediator between God and man. They called themselves *Unitarians.* This *intelligence universelle* is evidently the Logos, Rasit, or Αρχη or Buddha or Μητις.

It would seem probable that the followers of Bemrillah were originally adorers of Taurus, or the Calf or Calves, which they continued to mix with the other doctrines of Buddha. Much curious matter respecting these people, under the name of Druses, may be found in the third volume of the "Transactions of the Academy of Inscriptions," An. 1818.

Chaldean implies Sabæan. The word Chaldean is said to be a corruption of the word Chasdim; and this is most clearly the same as the Colida, and Colchida, and Colchis of Asia, and as the Colidei and Culdees of Scotland. Now all this, and the circumstances relating to the Chaldees, often called Mathematici, to the Assassins, the Templars, Manichæans, &c., being considered, the name of the Assassins, or Hassessins, or Assanites, or Chasiens, or Alchaschisin, will not be thought unlikely to be a corruption of Chasdim, and to

mean Chaldees or Culdees, and that they were connected with the Templars.   When the Arabic emphatic
article *al* is taken from this hard word *Al*-chas-
chischin, it is Chas-chis-chin.   The Assassins, were,
also, called Druses or Druiseans.   The learned author
of the " Celtic Druids" states that he has *proved* these
Druses to be both Druids and Culdees.   In all accounts
of the Assassins, they are said, also, to have existed,
in the East, in considerable numbers.   They are, also,
stated to have been found numerous by B. de Tudela*
not very far from Samarcand or Balkh ;—where he
also describes many great tribes of what he calls *Jews*
to live, *speaking the Chaldee language*, occupying the
country, and possessing the government of it.   He
says that among these Jews are disciples of *the wise
men*.   He says they occupy the mountains of *Haphton*.
Here are, it is to be thought, the *Afghans*, and that too
clearly to be disputed.   Under the word Haphton lies
hid the word Afghan, and the disciples of the *wise
man*, Hakem, frequented the Temples of Solomon in
Cashmere, &c., and were called Hkemites, Ishmaelians,
and Battenians, that is, Buddheans.   The word Hakem
is nothing but the word *hkm*, which in the Chaldee
means *wise*.   All physicians, in the East, are called
Hakem.   All this goes to prove that not only did
the Templars share doctrines with the Assassins and
Ishmaelians, but that they were much older than
the Crusades, and that the pretended origin of these
people is totally false.   The Gymnosophists, the
Kasideans, the Essenes, the Therapeutæ, the Dione-

sians, the Eleusinians, the Pythagoreans, the Chaldeans, the Assassins, and the Buddheans were all an order of religionists, including among them, and consisting in great part of, an order of Monks, who were, in fact, the heads of the society.

There is little doubt that all the Caliphs of the Saracens were, secretly or openly, Sophees. The Sophees are divided, at this day, into many sects, and, in their four stages, they have a species of Masonic, or Eleusinian, initiation from lower to higher degrees. Sir John Malcolm says, Hassan Sabah, and his descendants, were a race of Sofees, and that they were of the sect of Bâttaneâh, that is Buddha. They were Templars, or Casi-deans, or Chas-di-im, or followers of Ras or Masons.

The use of the Pallium, or sacred cloak, to convey the character of inspiration, was practised by the Imaums of Persia, the same as practised by Elias and Elishah (Eli-Shah). And it is continued by their followers to this day. When a person is admitted to the highest degree, he will receive the investiture with the Pallium and the Samach, which is the χειροτωνια. When the Grand-Seignior means to honour a person, he gives him a pellise, a Pall, a *pla*, a sacred cloak, a remnant of the old superstition, the meaning probably being quite forgotten. From this comes the word "palls" at our funerals.

One of the names, which excites the greatest curiosity as to its meaning, of the chief of the Assassins, was "Old Man of the Mountain"—*Senex de Montibus*. The Buddwa of Scotland was called "old man ;" and Buddha, in India, means *old man*. The opinion that the Assassins were Buddhists receives confirmation, in part, from the idea that he was reckoned as representative of the "ancient of days." The representative idea, or form, or figure by which the Prophet speaks of the Divine Intelligence—"Ancient of days," whose hair was wool, of a white colour. But in Persian, according to Sir John Malcolm, the word *Sofee* means both wisdom and wool. Is it possible that from this idea we obtain the white goats' hair cloaks of the Albanians, with their "snowy *camese* and their shaggy *capote;*" the white bernoose of the Moors, the white robe of the Carmelites: even the white uniforms of the Austrian army—nay, the sacred acceptation, and the supposed enchanted value, of the colour *white* generally?

That the renowned and dreadful tribes of Assassins, or Ishmaelites, whose history presents such an inextricable connection with that of the Templars, and also with that of the Hospitallers, were acquainted with, if not professors of the Fire-Creed of Zoroaster; from which, indeed, they were likely to derive their atheistic desperation; will be apparent when we examine the cruel and relentless stoicism of their fearfully blank belief. We suspect that these impassive and sinister (in the use thus made of them) doctrines not only underlie the philosophy of the directing chiefs of this abandoned body; these "offensive and defensive" associations of Assassins, who blindly had reposed all their reliance, and all their hopes, in the hands of their arch-priests as it were; but, further, we believe that there is (and always has been) a community of persuasions between the secret combinations of Arabia, Syria, and the other parts of the East, where bands of devotees and societies with secret teaching (as their base) existed, and the reflective, absorbed, abstruse and passionless atheism — interpenetrating and vivifying (if aught so dead could be, even, by "strange fire" vivified)—*Thuggee*. The *Thugs* are Epicureans and Quietests, stoical in their horrors (as there being no natural horror). Men who hold life as of no value—regard it as a weed. Enthusiasts who consider extirpation as a mere name :— nay rather, as the dutiful—though blind—aiding in the purposes of the gods. As in the idea of the Thugs and Assassins, or Ishmaelites, life is an evil, they benefit their victims, and act a dutiful part to God, in the scheme of the world, in removing them. Replacing them again, as it were, in the hands of the Divine ; who alone elected life as a place of bale.

What was really the object of the worship of the Knights Templars, in their secret synods, it seems very difficult to determine. Whether, indeed, in their intercourse with infidels, they had not imbibed some of the ancient, traditionary ideas, and learned the religion of the inhabitants of that part of Asia bounded by Persia, on the one hand, and by the Mediterranean on the other, seems a point more readily settled in the affirmative. In this view, flame-worship would have passed as a part of the adopted rites. We are thus brought to contemplate the Templars not so much in the light of a new superstition, as in the brilliancy of the philosophic positions of the Magi in the old world of thought, and of the Rosicrucians, Brethren of the Rosy Cross, or *Illuminati*, in the new.

Lamps and cloisters, lamps and altars, lamps and shrines, lights and tombs, are connected ideas. The romance lingering and brightening about which strange subjects may have its origin in the real, philosophic, unsuspected truth which gives life to their meaning even for all time. Romance never has life except for the truth which underlies it. With these fires among the graves—with the ultimate and funeral burning—with the *pyre* of the classics and the fire-immolations of the Orientals—with the sacred fire of the Magi, and the cressets and the torches of the Christian Knightly fraternities, we connect the ever-burning lamps, of which we have archæological accounts, and the suspected, Ishmaelitish, Bohemian or Fire-Worshipping Mysticism, harboured as the "strange thing" amidst the cowls and stoles, amidst the crosses and the books, and glancing, as the fiery crested snake, from among the resplendent arms of the supposed renegade Templars.

To this striking object of tomb-lights—incoherent in any other view than as the attestation, through the ages, of a universal, though a secret faith, Walter Scott accidentally (and unconsciously of its meaning) makes reference when he adjures the dying lamps as burning—

> "Before thy low and lonely urn,
>   O gallant chief of Otterbourne:
>   And thine, dark Knight of Liddesdale!"

Of the "grave of the mighty dead," Michael Scott, the wizard of such dreaded fame, he also says that, within it—

> "Burned a wondrous light;
>   Which lamp shall burn unquenchably;"

and that, when, in the moonlight, in the aisles of the
sainted Melrose, St. Michael's Cross of Red pointed,
amidst the slabs, to that "door of death" unloosened,
by the iron hand of Deloraine, from the ruptured
squares of the lettered pavement—

> " The light broke forth all gloriously ;
>   Stream'd upward to the chancel-roof,
>   And through the galleries, far aloof,
>   And, issuing from the tomb,
>   Show'd the Monks' cowl and visage pale,
>   Danced on the dark-brow'd Warrior's mail,
>   And kiss'd his waving plume."

The only serious hold which it is possible to
gain over the minds of men is through the influence of the supernatural.   It is absurd and inconsequential to believe that all the wonderful effects
which the Templars and the other Fraternities of
Devotees, which seemed bound by a religion produced
in their time, could have sprung from no higher motive
than the desire to aggrandise—to overpower—to rule
—to force.   Wonderful things—unbelievable things—
miraculous things—impossible things—must have been
offered to the common-sense of the men of the age,
before they would have given-in to the authority which
became to them as that of angels, of spirits, and of
the gods.   It is no slight task to master the resisting
common-sense of the world.   That which is invincible,
except at conviction.   Instincts at detection were as
strong then as now.   We are accustomed, every day,
to the infallible judgments of common-sense.   That
instant decision as to what a thing is, is as independent
of us as the sense of light.   Quick wits, sharp wits,

hardness of unbelief, suspicion, the same reason as is at work now—these were identical in the dark ages—in any age that man was man. Prophecy must have been wonderfully verified—the assumed magic must have been demonstrated real—something not at all a fraud—first, before imaginative and enthusiastic men, themselves, could believe it; second, before plain men could accept that which sense assured was impossible.

There must have existed in those secret societies, the dreams, trances, visions, magic-sight, which made princes of the seers. It is in this secret medium—whatever it may be—whether conjured out of the capacity of man in the intoxication of narcotics, through fumes, anointings, or lapsing out of the prisoned sense into the unimprisoned sense;—it is in their new world that the explorers stumble upon unbelievable, though real, things. Of a piece with the miraculous prevision obtained by the Grand Master of the Templars, in his agony, as noticed hereafter, must have been the two following instances of forecasting, which, as far as record can affirm them, are definitely established. The Priestess Phœnnis, the daughter of a Chaonic King, foretold the devastating march of the Gauls, and the course which they would take from Europe to Asia, together with the destruction of the cities, and this a generation before the event happened. So says Pausanias: xi., 12, 5. The King Pyrrhus had received an oracular sentence—that he was destined to die as soon as he had seen a wolf fighting with a bull. The sentence was fulfilled when, in the market-place of Argos, he saw a bronze group representing such a combat.   An old woman killed him by throwing down a tile from a house.

The Assassins, as a secret sect, had a kind of university among them.   The course of instruction in this university proceeded, according to Macrisi, by the following nine degrees.

The object of the first section of instruction, which was long and tedious, was to infuse doubts and difficulties into the mind of the aspirant, and to lead him to repose, with a blind, admiring confidence, in the knowledge and wisdom of his teachers.   To this end he was perplexed with extraordinary, and seemingly unanswerable, questions.   The absurdities of the literal sense of the Koran, and its repugnance to reason, were studiously pointed out.   Dark hints were given that, beneath the shell of the philosophy taught, lay a kernel sweet to the taste and nutritive to the soul. But all farther information was most rigorously withheld from the inquiring mind until the disciple had consented to bind himself, by a most solemn oath, to absolute faith and unreasoning obedience to his instructor.

In the second place, when the aspirant had taken the prescribed oath, he was admitted as a member of the second degree, which inculcated the acknowledgment of the particulars appointed by God as the sources of all knowledge.   This included science, and the arts and truths of life.

The third degree included the knowledge of farther important facts, and the connection, and succession, and power of those facts.   It also informed the student what was the number of the blessed and holy *imams*.

And this was the mystic seven; for as God had made seven heavens, seven earths, seas, planets, metals, tones, and colours, so seven was the number of the noblest of the angels, spirits, or attributes of God. Religion, as yet, was not outstept.

In the fourth degree, the pupil learned that God had sent *seven* lawgivers into the world, each of whom was commissioned to alter and improve, or rather to develope, the system of his predecessor; that each of these had seven helpers, who appeared in the interval between him and his successor: these helpers, as they did not appear as public teachers, were called the mute (*samit*), in contradistinction to the *speaking* lawgivers. The seven lawgivers were Adam, Noah, Abraham, Moses, Jesus, Mohammed, and Ismaïl, the son of Jaaffer; the seven principal helpers, called Seats (Soos), were Seth, Shem, Ismael (the son of Abraham), Aaron, Simon, Ali, and Mohammed, the son of Ismaïl. It is justly observed by the discerning Hammer that, as this last personage was not more than a century dead, the teacher had it in his power to fix on whom he would as the mute prophet of the present time, and inculcate the belief in, and obedience to, him of all who had not got beyond this degree.

The fifth degree taught that each of the seven mute prophets had twelve apostles for the dissemination of his faith. The suitableness of this number was also proved by analogy. There are twelve signs of the Zodiac, twelve months, twelve tribes of Israel, twelve joints in the four fingers of each hand, and so forth.

In the sixth place, the disciple being carefully led thus far, and his mind being duly prepared for what followed, the Koran, and the precepts contained in that book of authority, were once more brought under consideration, and he was told that all the positive portions of religion, and all the facts of faith, must be subordinated to the laws of nature and reconciled to the lights of philosophy, or be rejected as perhaps necessary to the apprehension, though intrinsically worthless.   In fact, man herein was thrown back upon nature, and taught to discover the exterior influences alone in it.   Then succeeded, for a long space of time, instruction in the systems of Plato and Aristotle.   When esteemed fully qualified, the scholar was admitted to the seventh degree, in which knowledge was imparted in that mystic Pantheism which is held and taught by the sect of the Sofees.   This was Bhuddism, without the supernatural light of Bhuddism.

As an eighth step into the *arcana* of philosophy, the positive doctrines of religion were considered in their light as a *necessity* to man, and as resulting from his position here in this world.   All the complicated knowledge which had now preceded was declared, in this forward stage of the student's progress, to be merely as the scaffolding by which the piling of the structure of real knowledge was to be effected.   All the builder's platforms and his poles, his work being now complete, were to be thrown down.   Prophets and teachers, heaven and hell, all the shows of life, its history, the machinery of the world, the human soul, were nothing.   Future bliss and future misery, reckoning for evil, conscience beyond the necessity of the maintenance of regularity in the world, aspiration for good out of the pleasant things of the world, justice and moderation beyond that common-sense of economy for the longer lasting, the intrinsic value of life, and the determent from the destruction of it other than in the policy of a certain blank atheistic "political economy"—all these were to be exposed as idle dreams, having nothing with the philosopher, whose sight had been cleared by a magic illumination, darkening or eclipsing, or overpowering, or *putting out* the false light of the world. Even as the light of day is drawn over the stars like a curtain.

In this absolute laying-level of the barriers of right and wrong, the point of view became consistent as showing that all actions should proceed, alone, from the centre point of self-pleasure in them, that power was right and that right was power, and that all laws were imported only into the world as securing the harmonious going on of it. That, in the absolute sense, there could be no such thing as sin; that therefore, in the absolute sense, there could be no such thing as punishment for it. Therefore, that nothing was to be feared on the score of conscience. Life was as a weed.

The ninth and last degree was that into which the disciple transcended (in this alarming sense), as seeing that, as nothing was to be believed, everything might be done.

Von Hammer argues an identity between the two orders, as he styles them, of the Ishmaelites and the Templars from the similarity of their dress, their internal organisation, and their secret doctrine. The colour of the Khalifs of the house of Ommiyah was white; hence the house of Abbas, in their contest with them, adopted black as their distinguishing hue. Hassan Sabah, when he formed the institution of the *Fedavee*, or the "Devoted to Death," assigned them a red girdle or cap. The mantle worn by the members of the Hospital was black.

The last Grand Master of the Templars, Jacques de Molay, together with his companion, Guy, brother to the Dauphin of Auvergne, were brought forth and placed upon a pile erected upon that point of the islet of the Seine, at Paris, where afterwards was erected the statue of Henry IV. It was a day of March—the 19th, as it is stated by the historians—1314. The two unfortunate Templars suffered with constancy, to the last asserting their innocence. The spectators wept and shrieked at the spectacle of their sacrifice. During the night their ashes were gathered up to be preserved as relics.

It is mentioned as a tradition in some of the accounts of the burning, that Molay, ere he expired, summoned Clement, the Pope who had pronounced the bull of abolition against the Order and had condemned the Grand Master to the flames, to appear, within forty days, before the Supreme Eternal Judge, and Philip to the same awful tribunal within the space of a year. Both predictions were fulfilled. The Pontiff did actually die of a colic on the night of the 19th of the following month. More dreadful still, the church in which his body was deposited, in state, took fire, the flames spread, and the corpse of Clement was

M

half consumed. The King, before the year had elapsed, by an accidental fall from his horse, suffered such injury that he, also, died. The fulfilment of these two prophecies produced great effect. The unfortunate Templars were almost regarded as martyrs.

It remains to glance at another singular point. We know that the general—nay, the universal belief is to the contrary—but has the Order of the Knights Templars, in a certain form, been continued down to our own day? That it has been so continued in a political fashion, and externally, there is no doubt, for the King of Portugal, in his dominions, formed the Order of Christ out of the Templars. The Freemasons, also, assert a connection with the ancient Templars; and there is a society, bearing the name of Brethren of the Temple, whose chief seat is at Paris, and its branches extend into various countries, and into England. It is asserted that Jacques de Molay, in the year 1314, in anticipation of his speedy martyrdom, appointed Johannes Marcus Lormenius to be his successor in his dignity, and that there has been an unbroken succession of Grand Masters down to the present times. That the secret doctrines of the Templars were partaken of by the Knights of the Order of St. John of Jerusalem, there appears to be but little doubt. Signor Rossetti, who possesses a very intimate acquaintance with the history of the Hospitallers, maintains stoutly that there is much in common between the doctrines taught in the higher grades of the Freemasons—more, also, that has been lost—and the views, *formulæ*, and fashions of the Order of the Temple. Lost in the clouds of antiquity, the dim forms of the mailed Templars disappear. Their buildings, their churches, their haunts remain. But the inhabitants are passed into the shadows. Their remembrance only survives in the quaint paved courts of the London Temple. The fact that their dwelling-place was once within the present purlieus of law— that the notes of their wild Eastern music, and that the ceremonies of their strange, scarcely Christian worship, were, in the time that has almost become a dream, real matters in the story of those, at present, so unromantic buildings—truths amidst this wilderness of mechanical law-spelling :—these things of a life, so unlike our present life, lend an interest to the very name of the Temple in Fleet Street. Fleet Street, with its bustle and its daily clocks! Fleet Street as we know it! Fleet Street of this very day!

It is stated, as something that we may believe, that there exist real, personal memorials of this antique and wonderful body of the Templars preserved, in secret, at the present moment, in Paris. Some of the archives and statutes—portions of the unexamined history— even a few of the mystic banners, and an assortment of the worn-out arms of the suspected brotherhood, still survive, it is said. These are declared still to lurk in some unknown and obscure corner of dilapidated buildings;—shut up hopelessly from modern sun, and denied even to the affectionate and indomitable inquest of antiquaries. Old Paris still caskets, we are assured, the mouldered remains of this once-puissant—nay, this princely association—this once glorious institution, founded on the centuries! In brief, it is confidently asserted that, even to this unbelieving, regardless, matter-of-fact nineteenth century, gloweth up still, some few faint, dusty gleams of a chivalry that once shook the world. That even to these contemporaneous days, and amidst our feet, start tokens most intimate and familiar of the long-buried soldiers of the Ruby cross—of mailed hermits, pilgrims, and banded guards of the Christian's holiest Jerusalem!

CHAPTER XIX.

POPULAR ANTIQUITIES IN THEIR CONNECTION WITH THE FIRE-PHILOSOPHY.

To this day in Sweden, on the first of May—the opening or germination of the year—the peasantry, as they do all over the North at certain times, light fires. A candle is lighted by all devout Catholics on Christmas Eve, and is kept burning, in memory and reminder of the mysterious Incarnation, until the dawning of the real day of the Blessed Nativity. The Yule-Log, whose bright-blazing is of so much moment, and with the last brand of which, most carefully and superstitiously laid aside for the purpose, the next year's Christmas Fire is to be lighted, follows the same rule. The Christmas Tree, the origin of which is lost in the mists of tradition, and which Teutonic emblem (time out of mind employed in Germany) is now transposed into England, though without the slightest suspicion of its Pagan meaning, is the mystic Northern sacrifice, and the attestation, in its multitudinous blazing candles, to the Genius or God of the Fire. The toys representing all the things of man, and of the earth, which are suspended, among the boughs, in its mythic light, are the sacrifice of all the good things of the world, and all the products of the Creative Fiat, as in surrender and acknowledgment, back to the Unknown Living Spirit, or Immortal Producer, who

hath chosen Fire as his symbol and his shadow.   This
is Baal worship.

If the reader will refer to the crest of His Royal
Highness Prince Albert, he will find the mystic, magic
horns distinctly set up.   The reproduction of the everduring symbol to which we have made frequent reference as recognisable as horns, wings, or otherwise in
the head-pieces of his ancestors of the North.   The
rough Runic soldiers who, in their barbarian incursions,
overturned (in the Roman beliefs), and buried in the
ruins of the Empire, a faith identical, in its secrets,
with their own.   All-ignorant of the fact that the
symbols of both spoke but the same tale, the original,
magic, Fire-Faith.   We have spoken of the horns,
ears, or *radii* of the Jester or Motley, as prevailing in
all places.   In the East, the idiot—"innocent," as he
is called in Scotland—has always been held in a
species of respectful distrust, or veneration, as—in his
very vacuity—the mouthpiece, or channel, of the
Outside Powers.   Sacredness attached to the "incapable," in the light of the soulless figure super-
naturally-motioned.   Deriveth the Jester his horns and
bells from this noblest of reasons?   Horns and bells
are found to decorate the Chinese and other Eastern
Idols—are also detected, in strangely-old, uncouth
missals, to form the appurtenances, even, of Saints.
What can all this mean?   What should it give, but
the obscure hint towards the universal tradition?
Bells are magical.   They "shake the spirit-spaces."
This is in the Rosicrucian mysticism.

The laurel-wreath around the head of heroes and
emperors—accorded alone to the great conqueror, the

Imperator, or the poet (majestic triplicate!), not only
mark out the line, and denote the place of the organs
of the highest intellectual and god-like faculties in the
brows of the human being, but prove the knowledge
of the ancients of phrenology, and represent the original
starry *radius*—that which symbolically invests the head
of all the gods.   It speaks the spirit-flame or *radius*—
magnetic and supernatural—intensifying to its real
magico-generative power in a circle of intolerable light,
about the head :—in which mystic light all magic and
sorcery, as well as all sainthood, was supposed, by the
Rosicrucians, to be possible, in accordance with the
laws of the supernatural Fire-World.   Crowns, garlands, wreaths, all the *insignia* of dignity that en-
circle the head; and all passing, be it remarked, over
the physico-phrenological places of the faculties of
" causality," " comparison," " wonder," " imagination,"
and in tracing them along, disclosing and glorifying
all the bodily points of the means of the greatness of
man ;—mitres and priestly head-coverings, the tonsure
of the sacerdotes, freeing the sacred circle of the
intellect (within which may the terrifically grand, very
apprehension of God, himself, be realised): from the
barbarian and the degraded—nay, brutelike growth of
hair, the very investiture and most closely branding
confession, and the complete and irresistible conviction, of the beasts—most abundant, and the grossest,
there where, in the scale, lowest ;—sceptres, wands,
priestly staves or crosiers, batons and maces :—all
these marks of rank, with the original disk, orb,
mound (or *mundus*), surmounting, with the mystic
symbol of the cross, the royal rods or sceptres of the

European monarchs :—all these forms are but the changes and reproduction of the rod of the Magician. He whose creed was the Fire-Creed, and whose secret means of working upon nature was the mysterious " sorcerer's sign," displayed upon, and through, the yielding magnetic worlds, deep through which stretched —he declared—the " shows" of the worlds, and converse with the real *substrata* of which, he pronounced, was by spells.   As spirit-visages were only to be won to the sight of, through enchantments.

The above are some of the ideas of the speculatists. It is curious how all these singular and picturesque notions intone and entwine, as it were, with all the grace, the beauty, the poetry, the romance, and the power in the world.   And how—realise, and utilise, and *demean* as we may—the mysterious and the wonderful, yet, are found to inform, stir, and to be the means of moving, as well as to the end of, everything.   For every solid, and the most prosaic, idea has some airy, and very romantic, notion which is the first starter of it.   The most worldly man's secret motive is sometimes the most inconsequential, and the most absurd one in the world.

It is surprising how many traces, to which we are altogether unconscious, even of the less old Pagan superstitions, not to speak of religious myths from India, still linger among us.   It is difficult to believe how they could have survived through the changes of the fashions ; and yet they do.   They have been reproduced through the generations, though now they are inconceivably faint.   And yet, to the archæological and learned eye, they are recognisable.   We will not speak of the Morris or Morrice dance (Moresque or Moorish), which used to be a favourite exhibition in our country-places; though we miss these quaint " Morris dances," everywhere, now. These singular dances, through which the little bells kept up a perpetual jingle, came circuitously to us from Spain, as bagpipes, out of Etruria, perhaps, found their way by the north. An acute author, who bestowed a lifetime on such investigations, assures us that the Druids were Masons, May's-sons, or devotees to Maia, *aia*, *ia*, or Io, the *Regina Cœli;* and that from long-descended tradition, and from the *Lingam* of India, came the May-Pole, the festival of the May-Queen (clad in white, and the daughter of the Pagan Io, as it were, and the representative of the opposite idea to the Lingam, the female principle, or nature, or Yoni of the Hindûs, the Io of the Egyptians, and the Ioni of the Greeks). From this seemingly most unlikely, but, in reality, undoubted root, comes the word C—ow, an animal which is, yet, an object of adoration in India. C-ow as I-ow.

Can it be that the old-fashioned perambulations, or processions, of the milkmaids, with flowers and garlands, on May-day, prevailing in London even until somewhat late in the last century, implied a far-off reference, not only to the mysteries of Venus, but to the festival of Io at the reopening of the year and the regeneration of nature? Does the ceremonial of "Going-a-Maying," and even the modern May-Day holiday of the Sweeps, mean the perpetuation, into the modern times, so very remote from its origin, of the Saturnian rout; with the clattered and barbarous shovels of the crowd of attendant sweeps, instead of the classic clash of the cymbals of the Corybantes :—

"Silver thrills of kissing cymbals,"

as the poet expresses it. Is it possible that we have the ancient myth, in our familiar London streets, on the annual May-Day; and that "Jack in the Green" (Bacche, Bacc, Iacche, Iacc, Iac, Jack) is meant for the God "Bacchus" (Taurus), or the Sun found in the *argha, arca,* ark, or "green," or bush, at the regeneration of nature or opening of the year? Perhaps the familiar phrase, "good wine needs no bush," may bear some distant import to this figure of the god "Bacchus" being found in a "bush." If this connection be correct, the sportive "Lord," as he is called, of the Sweeps may stand for the "Man," Mercurius, Hermes, or Thoth; and the "Lady" (Maid Marian, as she is commonly denominated in the *formula* of the old mysteries) may be no other than Io, Ia, Venus, or *Regina Cœli,* or the Sacred Cow of the Indians. How this *programme,* and this group of mythic and sacred personages, fell into the hands of the "Sweeps," it would be difficult to say : unless they stand as the legitimate successors, and representatives of the guardians of the fire, and of the murky, mystic workers in nature—the Cyclops. We may farther consider, in confirmation of our assumption, that there is mystic meaning in this Maytime sallying-forth of the Sweeps, that this "Lady," who may be none other than Dis, or Cybele, or the Virgin of the Zodiac, the Aphrodite of the Greeks, the

Astarte of the Phœnicians, or the triformed Luna)
(to whom our Saxon ancestors dedicated our Monday,
or Moon's-day), bears a golden ladle, as it is made to
be in the modern time; but in which, we think, we can
recognise the spear of corn or the magic reaping hook
of Ceres. And, in still farther mystic meaning, the
original *pedum*, the *lituus* of the Roman Augurs, the
Hieralpha of the Hindoos, and the rod which implies *divine* authority, and which is the means of all
enchantments.

In farther reference to these May-Day processions,
and in attempted elucidation of this unaccountable
masquerade of "Jack in the Green," as the centre
round which the celebrants are to dance, we may cite
the fact that the processions around the streets and
towns, in Catholic countries, are exact imitations of
those of the Pagans. When the Priests of the
Mother of the Gods made these processions through
the streets, they carried the image of Jupiter, which
they placed, for a short time, *in small bowers dressed
out for him*, precisely as is done, in Paris, at the *Fête-
Dieu*.

We recommend these suggestive points to the
notice of those who have closely examined the latent
truths which lie hid even in modern symbolism, and
who have attended to the nice shades of derivation.
There is no fund of more curious and profitable
research existing, than these singular affinities, and
long-inherited, religious meanings. By them we seem
linked more closely to the past. At first, vulgar
representative things, like those which we have
specified, seem impossible as the *media* of that they

are assumed as standing for. But possibility soon
glances on the mind. And the next feeling is one of
astonishment that myths could possess such inex-
tinguishable life. Their pliancy and accommodation
to new laws and circumstances—and yet, through all,
their invincible pertinacity—prove, if anything can
prove, that there is foundation for them in nature.
Through all, we descry the revelation, divinely
vouchsafed, for which we contend. All through its
mysterious complications and its adaptations, and (by
men) its corruptions, we can trace the unmistakable
signs of a direct divine revelation. And, totally
contrary to the opinions of the materialists, of whom
two-thirds of the thinking men, in modern times,
are unfortunately composed, revelation is the whole
scope and design of our book.

Anyone can perceive towards what end the
elaborate, mathematical refining and explaining away
of the idea of God, of the modern unconscious
materialists—who would resolve the Divine Being
merely into the harmonious operation of natural
laws, however overpoweringly sublime and perfect—
tends. It has been an effort, in our researches (and,
principally, in our application of them), to seek down
to the consummate; and, by the reason, alone, not-to-
be-contradicted plausibilities upon which men, in
their mathematical religious requirements, rely. We
think we have found, and taken the measurement of,
these invincible truths, painfully evoked, but triumphantly marshalled, in the operations of the reason.
And, after admitting all their conquering sharpness,
we decline to interchange, with these weapons,

implements of combat out of the same armoury. We think, in the celestial sword, we have discovered their master. We contest, as a total mistake, the ordinary philosophical arguments. Because we think there is a *farther* philosophy in which they are lost :— into which they all pass. This, then, is the higher knowledge. And, with inexpressible humility towards those truths which we desire to champion, we are seeking to convince back those who are filled with the desire to believe the old Bible truth :—if modern science, and the rationalism of the present days, will permit them. The belief of the supernatural is the only escape out of infidelity.

CHAPTER XX.

MYSTIC SYMBOLISM OF COLOURS.

PURPLE has been always the colour set aside, in the mysteries, as the mark of initiation;—as, in the higher grades, also of mastership. The Roman Augurs, than whom no class of men were held in greater veneration, as the means of the attainment to the knowledge of the purposes of the gods, were clothed in purple and in red. Hence, doubtless, the setting aside of this mystic colour, purple, for the robes of emperors and kings, who are supposed to be, or ought to be, the representatives of the great Thaumaturgists—are regarded as, in some sense, hierophants, or the possessors of hypernatural and transcendental knowledge:—the origin of kinghood in all ages. The colour ruby, or red, or intense carnation—or *inflammate sanguine*—follows the same law when employed in the pontificals of Roman Catholic prelates, the scarlet of the Princes of the Mother or Foundation Church, or the Cardinals, the red of British royalty, and of the English army, or even the vestments of the higher degrees in our Universities, whether the grades be clerical or lay. There is a certain shrouded, or emblemmed, meaning in these doctors' or teachers' or priestly colours, which claims the mysteries, and passes off, or up, into magic as their original. However little imagined this may be:—however little dwelt on, it may have been as conveying it.

What, again, is the signification of that grand traditional symbol of the White Horse, or Horse of Light of the Saxons, of which the original banner of the Saxon Conqueror of Britain, Hengist, the White Horse of Kent, the White Horse of Hanover, the White Horse, generally, of the Scandinavians stand witness? As also the colossal White Horse cut out and periodically restored and surviving from the very earliest and immemorial Saxon times, in England, down to our own day? Which horse any one may see displayed on the green, sloped side of that great hill in Berkshire; a considerable, low-lying district of which beautiful county bears the honoured, but not hitherto the satisfactorily accounted-for, name of the Vale of the White Horse. Concerning which maintenance, and effected at it, there happeneth, in that part of the country, a great festival, to which the neighbourhood crowds as to some religious service of even a paramount obligation. This gathering usually becomes as a very thronged fair. A recent book discourses very pleasantly, and with no inconsiderable instruction, upon this meeting, which is to periodically restore the " White Horse." In it, however, the author seems to have no suspicion of the portentous and prodigious character of the myth which the Berkshire White Horse probably celebrates and perpetuates. It would seem as the ever present, weird *hieroglyph* of the old Runic superstition, when there was really a powerful knowledge existent, unsuspected by the moderns. We take this colossal figure (in the Wolds of Berkshire) as the passing on, down into the ages, of an unwitted-of signal :—as a transmission, into the latter days, of the Brito-Saxon Palladium, or White Horse. The same deified emblem which is traceable all the world over. The same sign connecting the Magi and the moderns.

The connection of the revelation of spirits, in dreams, under the figures, or emblems, of "White Horses," has been pointed out in the earliest accounts of visions, and of nocturnal sleep-disclosures. We encounter them in the old Chaldean and Babylonish explanations of dreams, in those of the Hebrews, in those of the Egyptians, in those of the Greeks and Romans, in those of the lower Roman Empire, and in the monastic times. An analogy runs through all record of the kind. Perhaps the symbol of the Pale Horse, and of the "Death" to be mounted thereon, as shadowed forth in the Apocalypse, classifieth under the same head. And this which we cite below may, in some sort, be the original of the thing (whatever it distinctly be) meant, or signified, in this mystic emblem—so faithfully preserved—of the "Horse," or the "White Horse."

The idea of the fiery soul of the world—or the Binding Magnetism—which as the *last* of the physical, and the last possible thing to be known, Zoroaster, the supposed founder of the Religion of Fire, elevated into a god to be worshipped—this only, however, externally, in the visible sign of fire:—this idea, we say, we find mystically connected with the Horse, or the White or Lucent Horse. As thus. The Chaldean oracles of Zoroaster describe "a fire extending itself, by leaps, through the waves of the air. Or an unfigured fire, whence a voice runs before. Or a light beheld near, every way splendid, resounding and con-volved. Also a *horse full of refulgent light.* Or a boy carried on the swift back of a horse, fiery, or clothed in gold, or naked ; or shooting an arrow, and standing on the back of a horse. Such things do not portend change in the divine nature itself, which is one; but they show how variously it is participated by intellect, the rational soul, phantasy, and sense. To the pure intellect it is seen impartibly. That is, it is at one, outside—as we may say—*man.* Who, outside of his own nature, is at one, also, with it. But, descending, it expands, assumes figures, &c. Homer says, the gods, when clearly seen, are overpowering; and one of the deities is made to say, " The miserable heart, by whom I am received, cannot bear me." In a word, the gods appear to be changed when the same divinity appears according to different orders, descending into subject distinctions. For, the fables then represent one and the same divinity, assuming those various forms into which it makes progression.

We may, *en passant*, recall to the reader that, in India, the sacrifice of horses, and, in particular, of white horses, has been a favourite method of propi-tiation ; that in Japan the same idea prevails, as also in China. The sacredness of the White Elephant, and the quasi-worship of it in Asia, and the mystical idea, generally, of the sacredness of the colour white, may, also, trace from this source. The horses that drew the chariot of the hero, in the Roman triumph, were always white. The state horses of the King of Hanover, in memorial of the magic idea connected with the White Horse of Hengist, were white. The horse of the conqueror has commonly been white by choice. White is the colour for virgins; hence it is the nuptial colour. It has its origin in the magic sacredness. It means magic. White was the colour for penitents, as their being, for the moment of their expiation, in another world. The taper held in the penitent's hand was the witness-light to the Fire-Religion, of the univeral tokens of which, we can move but a very little way out into the world without encountering some one. It is extraordinary how very widely scattered are the symbols, and, yet, how very little notice any of them attract.

Scattered all over the world, as we have repeatedly said, are traces of a primeval people, who, to all our thoughts of them, seem to have possessed a knowledge greater than man can contemplate as ever owned by him. Wonders seem to have been familiar to these early dwellers upon the earth. Where could have been their seat—from whence they could have come—how their knowledge could have been derived, otherwise than through some supernatural disclosure;—how they vainly strove to perpetuate, and to place upon indelible record, their religion—how they moved and wandered—how all history sank off from the commemoration of them, and how their very mightiest landmarks were engulphed, and have all but disappeared, in the rising tide of the accumulating centuries:—how all this should be, and be so little supposed, is a profound speculation of the modern time. The *lithoi* that are found studding numerous countries, ancient and modern, attest the existence, in a most remote period, of some extraordinary and unaccounted-for race. With infinite labour, and with the most singular and happy ingenuity, one antiquary has followed up all the traces of this lost race, until he settles them as in the very heart of the world, or in the middle of Asia. Let us listen to what this indomitable elucidator has to tell us of these fathers of mankind.

" In the old books of the Hindoos, as it was before stated, we meet with accounts of great battles which took place between the followers of the Linga and those of the Ioni, and that the latter, in very early times, were expelled from India under the name of Yavanas. After the sun had left Taurus and entered Aries, or about that time, it is probable that the war above alluded to arose. Whether the question of the precedence of the Linga and Ioni had any connection with the transit from Taurus to Aries I know not, but the two events appear to have taken place about the same time. The Buddhists or Yavanas were expelled; their priests were Culdees; and they were Jaines. They passed to the West. In their way they built, or their sect prevailed in, the city of Baal, Bal, or Babylon—as Nimrod says, probably the old Iona:

"' Et quot *Iona* tulit vetus, et quot Achia formas.' *

They built, or their sect prevailed in, the cities of Coan or Aiaia, if ever there were such cities—the city of Colchis or of the Golden Fleece, if ever there was such a city, to which the Argonauts are feigned to have sailed—the city of Iona, which afterwards became Antiochia—and the city of Iona, called afterwards

* Nimrod, vol. i., p. 287.

Gaza, where they were Palli or Philistines, and near to which Jonas was swallowed up by a whale—and the city of Athens, called Athena (a word having the same meaning as Iona), with its twelve states and Amphictyonic council. They dwelt in Achaia, they built Argos, they founded Delphi, or the Temple of the navel of the earth, where they were called Hellenes and Argives. They founded the state of the Ionians, with its twelve towns in Asia Minor. They built Ilion in Troy, or Troia or Ter-ia, *i.e.*, country of the Three. They carried the religion of Osiris and Isis, that is, Isi and Is-wara, to Egypt. They took the deity Janus and Jana or Iana to Italy, where their followers were called Ombri. They founded the city of Valentia, or the city of Rama or Roma. They built Veii, or the city of Uei (read from right to left Ieu, if ever there was such a city).

"Passing farther to the west, and arriving in our own neighbourhood, they built the Temple of Isis, now called Notre-Dame, or the Queen of Heaven, at Paris; and, as it might be called, Baghis-tan, now St. Denis, and were called Salarii from their attachment to and practice of the sacred mazy dance. They left the Garuda at Bordeaux. They founded—in Britanny— the most stupendous monument, called Carnac, of the same name * as the Temple of Carnac in Egypt, and the Carnatic in India. They built Stonehenge, or Ambres-stan, and Abury or Ambrespore. They founded Oxford, on the river which they called Isis, and Cambridge, on the river Cam, Cham, *Ham*, Am,

* See "Celtic Druids."

or Om. They built Iseur or Oldborough (Aldborrough) in Yorkshire, and called the Yorkshire river by the name *Omber* or Umber or Humber, and called the state, of which Iseur was the capital, Brigantia, the same as the state which they had left behind them in Spain or Iberia, and Valentia a little more to the North, and Valentia in Ireland, the same as the Roma and Valentia in Italy and Spain. And finally, they founded a College on the island of Ii or Iona, or Columba, which remained till the Reformation, when its library, probably the oldest in the world, at that time, was dispersed or destroyed." It is, however, suspected that part of this invaluable library, which had been copied through generations, at the dissolution of the monastery, went to Douay in Flanders.

"These were the people," resumes the author, whom we have quoted above, "Jains or Buddhists, whom, in my 'Celtic Druids,' I have traced from Upper India, from Balkh or Samarcand, one part between the 45th and 50th degree of North latitude, by Gaul to Britain and Ireland, and another part by sea, through the pillars of Hercules, to Corunna, and thence to Ireland, under the name of Pelasgi, or sailors of Phœnicia."

CHAPTER XXI.

SYMBOLISM AND THE SUPERNATURAL.

THE Snake, Serpent, Dragon, is a universal emblem in all Mythology : glancing up to us in the religions of all nations ancient and modern, Christian as well as Heathen. There must be something infinitely farther meant in this than is supposed. There must be some occult truth bodied forth in this strange symbol that has never yet been discovered. The monuments of Egypt, the marbles of Greece, the *tympana* and architectural ornaments of the Romans in farther-off hints, the lonely monuments in the Scythian wilds, the uncouth fragments of the buried cities of Central America, the starry courts (with their reduplicate *arabesques*) of the Alhambra, the theistic memorials of the Persians, that fantastic templar-piling of the Chinese, the almost wind-shaken, belled pagodas of China, itself, the elephantine structures of Hindoostan, the shattered palace-turrets of Delhi, alike give—in innumerous forms—this mysterious glyph of the "Snake." Its uncertain imprint haunts the Kremlin, glows to a sort of furtive light amidst the mosque-like cupolas of the holy Kiew. The figure lurks in the old Runic stones, the expression of this wonder glances up from amidst the table-monuments of the chapels of the minster, is shadowed amidst the buttresses of cloisters, soliciteth to the observer from the feet of gilt, brass, or stone

effigies, where, pierced with the point of sword or
butt of crosier (the ancient *pedum*), or pressed down
by sandaled, or by mailed, or by slippered foot, it
glanceth to the student's recognition in the shape of
dog, or in some semblance, however remote, of the
" four-footed." The creeper gifted with the power
of flight.

Great things are buried. In all substantial, eternal
matters, the past is immeasurably the superior of
the present. Our modern knowledge is the wreck of
the mighty knowledge of the time that has gone.
Contemporaneous man—except in his conveniences—
is the shadow of the ancient man. What if this
myth of the " Snake" shall express some vital,
necessary, extra-natural and eternal truth? In our
suspicion, it should seem to do so. What if the
Snake, Serpent, Dragon, Fish, Egyptian Apis or
Bull, Indian Cow, Golden Calf of the Israelites,
Uræus, Goat, the " Horned Creature" generally,
Magic Horse, or reptile, or horizontal "Locomotive,"
unilluminate Organism, or moving clay, in opposition
to the Vertical Ray, or the idea of the Presence of
God, be all one? What if all shall be only the
varying expressions of the same Myth? What if
thus be hidden the unpronounceable, tremendous,
and secret truth; which has in the past time, is,
and ever must be concealed in the darkness of the
mysteries and guarded by priests and Magians, and
be virtually, and vitally, and of God-denial to him,
not for man? If this awful distrust (in the good
sense) of the constitution of things be really truth,
we gain at once Revelation and Godhood. And, as

the second conquest—springing from the first as
light chaseth darkness—we philosophically annihilate
Atheism.

"I, indeed, baptise you with water, unto repentance," saith Saint John. "But he that cometh
after me is mightier than I; whose shoes I am not
worthy to bear. He shall baptise you with the Holy
Ghost, and *with Fire*."

What is the meaning of this?

Is the Pythagorean Evolvement or Transmigration,
the Hindoo *Maia*, the Catholic Purgatory, the heathen
Tartarus and Hades, the Christian Hell, the sectarian
and unexplained Limbo, shadowed-forth, or dimly
and fitfully gleaming up to comprehension in all this?
That which we seek to educe is the necessity of the
Supernatural:—is the absolute fact of the Vital
Religion, really, about us; though we know it not,
and will deny it. Shall the meaning and purpose of
incense in worship, and of those magic clouds of the
fragrant and trance-creating fumigations which then
invest the worshipper be the evolvement of naturally
inner clear-seeing, supernatural worlds, through which
we must make our way to Heaven? Shall these
exalted, divine lines of beams be as the spires of gold,
to radiate, as out of our centrically-excited, own,
possible spot of Holy Fire, into that eternal, matter-
less, New-Jerusalmen of intolerable God's Light?
Shall the mystic significance, and glorying and
rescuing object of the *Viaticum*—blessedest and most
sacred of man's means towards it—be as the snatching
past the, otherwise, inevitable, transcendental, purgatorial, rings of inferior states of being—cycles of

even unconscious dole—of the sinking Human Soul? Rapt as by the Angels, fleet from the floor of Heaven, and brightest from the lowest "Steps of rows of stars" of the Throne of God? May this trance of the Magians be the setting-aside of the chosen one, or of the Elect, to whom shall be presented the supernatural scenes, for whom shall, even to his man's capacity, be interpreted the unbelievable wonders, and to whom, in his triumphant treading of the denials of reason, shall be opened the chance of the Kingdom of God? May this be, also, the object mystically sought (however never gained, save by Saints) in—correctly looked-at—the occult rite of consecration; embalming with oil?

For as the first kings—inasmuch as the earliest rulers of men—were demi-gods, consecrated in their supernatural rings of glory, or of the holy fire, so the children of God, or the first priests, were Saints. Those whose very *nimbus* of martyrdom was as their crown of majesty. Sainthood is the true earliest title of kingship. It has come out of the supernatural. The first of kings have ever been the first of magicians. This is the only true title to be great and mighty among men. From the supernatural can only come the gifts of the supernatural—which are right, justice, and power. The earliest kings were kings of mind.

The foregoing are the sublime views of the Rosicrucians concerning the mysteries. There is much deep mysticism in them, and they are difficult to be understood. But the consideration of them opens a highly refined philosophical and theological field. We have sought, throughout our book, to explain these exceedingly difficult-to-be-comprehended and singular views in as direct and simple terms as we could command; commensurately with the inherently shadowy nature of that which we sought to interpret.

It will never do to urge that these things lie beyond us. A fruitful source of the spiritual lowness of the modern time, is the resolute averting of the face from deep thoughts, which, of course, give trouble. That all the lifting of the mind, that all the sublimest speculation, that all the occupancy of the thoughts by these intensely noble and refining investigations—that all these high ideas, and great ideas, about God's providence, and His purposes in the world, end when pushed to answer, just where they began—that is, where they first opened, and in nowise attaining to definite result: this is, of course, as true as that men cannot help their speculations and their wonder. But we unconsciously pass higher, and become something better, in such thoughts. We teach ourselves to place the world at a distance. We grow spiritualised; and the very amount of our pleasures multiplies because it purifies. The fault of the time is haste—is conceit—is a wilful disregard of the higher truths—is a protesting speed to be back again amidst the business of the world—a cowardly acknowledgment of incapacity to cope with the contemplation of man's possible higher destiny—a hypocritical putting-forward of reliance upon, and acknowledgment of, a beneficent superintending Providence in the abstract. This time is so unenthusiastic, everything is so questioned for its utilities, and all so toned down to commonplace, that it is the voice of exclamation, and *alarm*, only, that can arouse. To obtain a hearing we must call aloud.

We are involving ourselves in too many deductions. We are thickening ourselves in our mechanical dreams too much. We are posing ourselves with systems. We are living the heart out of us. We are making very clockwork of the grand intensities of nature. Formalism is becoming as a second nature to us, and our method of living is the translation of the life-long charities into pounds and pence. Even our very fine cases—as we may so, perhaps, too " curiously" figure it—are growing vastly too fine, vastly too wonderful and too elaborately wrought for us. Why not be of rougher material, and of mere painted outside—of bulk and not sentiment—of the coarse, solid components—of wood and of varnish— instead of making up of such exquisite vermilion blood, and of flesh of a marble-like whiteness in the female examples of us? There be something in superb colours, look you! Why, when we are so laboriously casting ourselves as into ingots for the devil's golden Hades, should we make all this hypocritical fuss about moral improvement. Surely we might as well become stumps—blocks:—turn into dead, hard wood, as mean and unhandsome as Lapland idols, when all our foolish pity, and all our human sympathies, are being most convincingly argued, and demonstrated, out of us; and when the very affections are strangled—Oh, think us not too direct and plain-spoken, our dear, contented, but, perhaps, too compliant reader—like irregular children; those which are only sure to bring their parents into discredit. Children of no parish, since they belong not to a parish where money abounds! Owning no love, since they cannot claim affinity with the love of bank-notes!

We have forgotten the inside of the cup in the burnishing of the exterior. Nor—after all—do we live half our life. Our triumphs in the common conveniences of life—spite of our vaunting of our perfection in them—go not great lengths. We can forge an anchor. But we cannot cook a dinner. We can spin thousands of yards of calico in two or three revolutions of a wheel. But we, personally, curve so indifferently, that we can scarcely make a bow. The banks groan with our gold. And yet we have not the knowledge profitably—by which we here mean towards our soul's advantage—to expend a single shilling. In this universal Plutus-conversion, our heads—so to speak—are growing into gold, while our hearts are fast becoming but as the merest blown paper-bag inside of us!

Is this Dutchlike life of toys and trifles right? Is this all of nature;—and all of us? Oh this wilderness of flowers, and oh, the eternal forests! Let the mind, for a moment, glance at that inexpressible microcosm—far from the vulgar disturbances of the pavements, and out of sight of the glare of the city—in which are the thin spiry stalks, in whose invisibly minute veins course up the bright-green blood. What a neglected treasury is this world of ours, in which lie undreamt of riches for the seeking! Why abandon them all—desireless—to the inviting angels?—who stand sentinels upon a Paradise upon which we might enter! Oh those countless diversities, and for ever sumless beauties of nature! Oh—stretching above us—all ye vast fields! Blue as the very ultimate floor of divinity:—throbbing with worlds, as through the intensity of an all-exultant, all even violently God-declarant life! Oh all ye thousand visible wonders, that scatter spells, as of the fruitful magic, through all this most invisibly populous universe; this universe, whether of man's mind or of the larger macrocosm! Pronounce, ye that know, whether evil, meanness, or wresting to false purpose:—whether aught of bad—should profane a theatre of grandeur so immense? Is not man, himself—who ought to be the arch-glory, as the *recognition* of it—but as he would seem so desirous of making himself—the blot upon this excellence, the lie to all this overpowering sublimity? Is he not, himself (to speak to him the language which he may best understand), the *bankrupt* in this myriad of banks, whence thought can—and virtue might—draw their inexhaustible supplies?

Were gold-ribs the very framework of the world, and were they torn out of their mighty sockets; were even the Genius of its Riches shown, barless and central, throned at the very heart of this so detestably, because so for its material glory, worshipped globe: —would the sight (or the possession) match against thine immortal chance? Were the spirit of the material world exposed, in a single revelation, in all his blasting splendours, would, oh thou miserably

merchandising heart! thou seller of thy seat amidst
the star-girt saints! thou wretched contemner of the
chance offered thee, for thy salvation, by thy God!—
would all this compensate for the averting, for one
moment, from thee, of the face of the Rulers of thine
immortal destinies? Confess, thou mad and besotted
man!—avouch, thou less defiant than hypocritical rebel
to God's heavenly care of thee!—would thy very
hugest heap of dross match in value with the tiniest
flower, into whose thirsty cup the heaven-missioned
spirit poured his eternal dew? Christening to immortality?

Boastest thou of thy world, and of thy dignity—
in thy science—out of it? Art!—what is art to the
fine-spun tracery of the meanest moss? Labour—
what is thy labour, that thou shouldst pride thyself
upon it—when the whole frame of stars be nightly
moved? Pride!—why, what a shallow thing is this
pride, when to the lily of the field even Solomon, in
all his glory, has been declared not equal! What be
thy stars and ribbons—thy rings and spots—when,
than all, the snake hath more splendid? What be
thy traceries, and all thine ingenious adornment, when
the summer insect—less than thee the "painted child of
dirt"—surpasseth thee at them? What be thy money,
when, with whatever assurance thou reliest upon it,
it may not spot for thee, as gold nails, thy final,
melancholy, and long-lasting house? Hoarder for
that day of enjoyment which shall never come to thee,
in thy last home, all thy tenfold fences of precious
metal useless, art thou content to put-up with most
ignoble lead! Thou leavest all thy wealth, all "thy

goods and chattels," and, for aught thou knowest, thou forfeitest thy very soul; and at that, perhaps, terribly sudden summons, thou stand'st not even solitary! For is there not thy misspent life, thee to confront? Thou hast bargained away thine heritage, and hast spent the price, and, now, as that as which to be it hath been thy greatest boast—a good "man of business"—thou must, in rendering up thyself, perform thine own half of the obligations. If the real law be that life to come be alone purchaseable by good deeds—as any lawyer will tell thee, friend, if thou consultest him—thou hast miscalculated the law. In thine own interest's sake, then, better a single virtuous act than a reiteration of money-victories! Better, for thee, the prayer of the poor man, and the blessings of the fatherless and of the widow, than a whole shipload of plate, an *avenue* of bowing menials, and a whole court of flatterers! Remember that the reckoning, with thee, must come. Disencumber yourself in time. Perhaps the very " conveyances of thy lands" may not be contained in that box, in which there will be found, at last, but too much room for the possessor himself!

Art thou wise—even in this world's sense? Art thou sagacious as to the relative meanings of " debtor and creditor?" When all the world attesteth that these things are true, *shalt* thou, then, persevere in so hopeless a chase of phantoms—of fine false things which flee from thee! Shalt thou, with this knowledge, strain for an imagined good, which, even in thine own hand, melteth? Shalt thou, with all these results, which experience avoucheth as imminent, still

sleep the sleep of fools? Still, with no alarm, fold
the accustomed hands, and acquiesce because we see
all the world doing so likewise! Shalt thou waste thy
precious hours in the pursuit of those anticipated fine
things, which, for all thy knowledge to the contrary,
are to prove as daggers to thee? If missing *thee*,
perhaps to prove nets to the feet to trip up, or pits of
selfishness, or of mistake, into which they shall fall, to
those to whom thou leavest thine accumulation! That
for which thou canst have no farther use, keep it as
tenaciously as thou mightest want! Those that thou
fanciest best beloved, may but inherit direct ruin in
heiring thy riches. That which might have been as
a gold mosaic pavement for thee to walk over in thy
lifetime, may, in the sinking under thee in thy final
disappearance out of this slippery world, convert as
into a devil-trap to thy children!

Love not money, then, other than "wisely;" and
not "too well." Grow back into the simplicity of
thy childhood. Time hastens from thee. Thou, really,
hast not that half-century which thou proposest to live.
Live at once; in leading a new life. Prate not in thy
vanity, but get thyself to thy knees, thou foolish man!
And confess thyself a very child—in the true wisdom.
Recall thy mind to better things than thy wretched
traffic in which by far too much thou imitatest the
muck-worm. Make much of the holy affections which,
like flowers, Heaven hath planted in the mind of thee
(if thou, like an ox, wouldst not tread them so daily
out with thy brutish feet); and of thy children. Each
of thine innocent little children contradicteth thee.
Thine own youth is that which the most completely

exposeth thy false policy. Think that thou hast but the poorest portion of life. Thy widest margin of profit, and thy very mound of bonds and of bank-notes, alike shall prove but clogs—aye, but as tons of dead weight—in the hour when unexpected affliction shall start up before thee, or in that time that thou hast thy real summons out of this world. Chains are wealth :—aye, chains of heaviest link ; hell-forged, but self-wound in one's unconsciousness of acquisition—of which for its escape, in the last hour, the angels have, perhaps, to free the struggling soul ! The blessing of the orphan, and of the widow—of the lately down-trodden, but the, now, rescued—shall be the wings upon which, in triumph out of thy clay, shalt thou mount to the face of God ! Then to thy heart shall penetrate, and to thine ears shall reach, that blessed assurance, welcoming thee within the doors of the eternal places:—"Even as thou didst it to the meanest of these thine earthly brethren, hast thou done it unto me !"

The roads to Heaven, out of this mere miserable, transitory man's world—this world of disputes and difficulties, of the struggle, and of the eagerness to live, but of the compelled and confused haste when death arrests—this place of weariness and discomfort, of—in the real reasons of things—very frequently, the high-placed low, and of the lowly-placed high : the ways, leading beyond those clouds of heaven towards which thou gazest, thou longing man ! have not those solid barriers of division, between body and spirit, which thou sometimes art taught to believe ! Look out into the universe—important as thou thinkest thine own globe—and imagine what innumerable

o

"mansions" thy "Father's house" hath. By how many ways may the hope (which may be all of thee) travel into the celestial spaces! By how many natural and ethereal wickets the blessed may, according to their natures, enter! Are not the stars as bright doors, opening into the glory?

"God called up from dreams a man into the vestibule of heaven, saying, 'Come thou hither, and see the glory of my house.' And to the servants that stood around his throne, he said, 'Take him, and undress him from his robes of flesh: cleanse his vision, and put a new breath into his nostrils: arm him with sail-broad wings for flight. Only touch not with any change his human heart—the heart that weeps and trembles.'

"It was done; and, with a mighty angel for his guide, the man stood ready for his infinite voyage: and from the terraces of heaven, without sound or farewell, at once they wheeled away into endless space. Sometimes with the solemn flight of angel-wing they fled through Zaarrahs of darkness, through wildernesses of death that divided the worlds of life; sometimes they swept over frontiers, that were quickening, under prophetic motions, towards a life not yet realised. Then from a distance that is counted only in heaven, light dawned, for a time, through a sleepy film. By unutterable pace the light swept to *them*, they by unutterable pace to the light. In a moment the rushing of planets was upon them: in a moment the blazing of suns was around them. Then came eternities of twilight, that revealed, but were not revealed. To the right hand and to the left towered mighty constellations, that by self-repetitions and by answers from afar, that by counter-positions, that by mysterious combinations, built up triumphal gates, whose architraves, whose archways—horizontal, upright—rested, rose—at altitudes, by spans—that seemed ghostly from infinitude. Without measure were the architraves, past number were the archways, beyond memory the gates. Within were stairs that scaled the eternities above, that descended to the eternities below. Above was below, below was above, to the man stripped of gravitating body. Depth was swallowed up in height insurmountable, height was swallowed up in depth unfathomable. Suddenly as thus they rode from infinite to infinite, suddenly as thus they tilted over abysmal worlds, a mighty cry arose—that systems more mysterious, worlds more billowy—other heights, and other depths—were dawning, were nearing, were at hand.

"Then the man sighed, stopped, shuddered and wept. His overladen heart uttered itself in tears; and he said, 'Angel, I will go no farther! For the spirit of man aches under this infinity. Insufferable is the glory of God's house. Let me lie down in the grave, that I may find rest from the persecutions of the Infinite! For end, I see, there is none.' And from all the listening stars that shone around issued one choral chant:—'Even so it is! Angel, thou knowest that it is. End there is none that ever we yet heard of!' 'End is there none?' the angel solemnly demanded. 'And is this the sorrow that kills you?' But no voice answered, that he might answer himself! Then the angel threw up his glorious hands to the heaven of heavens, saying, 'End is there none to the universe of God? Lo, also, THERE IS NO BEGINNING!'"

CHAPTER XXII.

MAGICAL CEREMONIES AS A MEANS OF COMMUNICATION BETWEEN THE SEEN AND THE UNSEEN.

DOES this charming out of the world, by magical applications, mean converse with the power outside, for which there are no fleshly chains? Are, in short, these coronation rites, dedication ceremonies, inauguration-forms—are these unguents, and this balm, is this anointing and incensing but the magic-seeking to stop up the senses, as we may say, and to throw open the doors of a new life to evolve out of this life? Laying the bridge from the state visible to the state, in this life, unknown?

Is this that Jacob's Ladder up which, and down which, he saw the angels (or spirits) ascending and descending, as from the glories of the courts of heaven into the mists of earth? And urging up the stairs of light of which, supernaturally in the divine *afflatus*, we are alone, to attain to the feet of God? If Bible-truth mean anything, it surely meaneth this!

Throughout Hindostan, a practice never omitted, is to carve out a small niche in every grave, and therein to place a lamp, which is carefully tended. In the Jewish persuasion every follower of the law—nay every Hebrew, however lax in other respects he may persistently be, and however indifferent to his religion—on the anniversary of the death of his parent lights up and maintains, a lamp from the sunset of the day before until the dawn of the day of the death. We believe this rite has been preserved in unbroken continuity, and that, by all zealous Jews, it is still regarded as a mystic obligation, to slight or neglect which would be more than blameable, inasmuch as it would be the precursor of misfortune—of great trouble.

Here is a singular votive resemblance to the Roman-Catholic practice on the Eve of the Blessed Nativity. "Ganga's lamp," set adrift and watched, as it burns floating on the stream, and the extinguishment of which is a matter of the most inauspicious import, and of the deepest grief, to all devoted Hindoo maidens (as also of their lovers), is a well-known superstition. Both the maiden and her lover are represented as engaging in the same act at an identical, predetermined moment; and their future fates are supposed to be indicated either by the clear-burning of the lamp until it passes out of sight, or by its premature extinguishment. This superstitious practice ranges under our diverse catalogue of fire-sympathies, of fire-usages, and of fire-emblems. However remote it may seem, tonsure, in general, is undoubtedly indicative of the same occult observance. In the West and North, and under the Christian dispensation, it has shrunk into a mere practice, among the priests, of shaving the crown of the head. But in the East,* as we see among the Chinese, and as

---

* Tonsure of the priests and monks is an exact imitation of that of the priests of Isis. Apuleius, "The Golden Ass."

prevailing with other peoples, whole nations have subscribed to this singular, emblematic custom, rite, sacramental practice, or whatever it may be denominated. In fact, the usage, unexplainable and incoherent under any other theory, becomes consistent, and seems like reason, when viewed in this light of the sanctification of the head in the assumption of the traditional, earliest divinity of fire. We mean that there is indicated in it a magnetic, sacred polarity of the human being. The tuft of hair on the head of the faithful follower of Mahomet, whilst all the rest of the head is shaven close, and the long, dependent, most superstitiously regarded, and solicitously preserved and defended, *queue* of the natives of the Celestial Empire, may, in their origin, have been intended to signify the vertical flame, or the "God-chosen man." We take also architecturally, as it were, from the expression and look of the adjunct, the *acroterium*, or pedimental honour-point—to speak in the heraldic phraseology of it—of the classic, triangular closing of the roof, or of the pediment or pyramid—as also the splayed *stele* at its either angle—as indicating, and as imitative of, *flames*, and therefore as speaking, although so unsuspectedly, of the mysteries, and of the first, and noblest, and holiest religion of the Holy Spirit. Heathen as these latter exemplifications and tokens of it may seem to be. They are not so, however.

If the bond of the whole visible world be the universal magnetism, then the immortal, unparticled Spirit, of which this magnetism is the shadow, may be that ineffable potentiality, in which the real religion

shall be alone possible. In this manner shall
Sainthood be true of all time. In this " new world
of the old world," shall miracle be possible. In
this manner, out of the familiar shall come the wonderful. In this angelic medium shall Heaven rest!
And alone rest.

CHAPTER XXIII.

CHRISTIAN OBSERVANCES IN THEIR CONNECTION WITH THE FIRE-PHILOSOPHY.

In the Catholic ritual, Candlemas-Day, or the Purification, is a celebration and grand presentation of lights, following, and consequent upon, the festival of the Holy Nativity. It was the practice, and the enjoined duty, in the old days of the Catholic faith, for women, at that which, in the Protestant Church, is called the Churching after childbirth, to offer an acknowledgment of candles. We may all bring to mind, in illustration, the fierce message of William the Conqueror, in 1087 (the year of his death), to the King of France, who ventured an unseemly but pointed jest on his confinement to bed, and on his corpulence. "Tell the King of France, from me," cried the incensed William, "that, at the time proper for such appearance, I shall not only be up, but that, at my churching, I shall present so many and such terrible lights as shall set the whole kingdom of France in flame!" And the King kept his word; though at the cost of his own life, as history avoucheth. The manner of his death is well known. Ravaging and burning all before him, at the town of Mantes, which he had just destroyed, his horse happened to place his fore-feet on some hot ashes, causing a sudden jerk forward, on the pommel of the saddle, to the rider. Being in a bad state of health, the bruises which he received induced a fever, of which King William shortly died. Thus the angry monarch's death was indirectly of fire of his own raising. Retribution for such blind revenge at so poor a joke.

Now, finally, we may thus sum our historical examination. That, at every turn of our inquiry, we meet light. At every cross-road, as it were, of our laborious journey—of our philosophical pilgrimage—we encounter this pertinacious and ever-following Light. We have seen that not only at birth, but as taking a prominent part in the torch-celebration at marriage, and again, and more impressively, at death and in the ceremonials of sepulture, the phantom of light never fails. It the more dimly or the brighter—the more gloriously and the more cheerfully celebrant, or the more awfully full everywhere discloses. As everything, it must—though disguised—be everything. What may mean this concentrate, Resplendent Figure? This ever-following myth? This ever-recurring suspicion of a tremendous thing? This terrible, and yet this greatly grand angel, found at the couch-side at our birth, accompanying us, as the best and the most distinct sacrifice, to the altar of presentation, where our mother bows in her thanksgivings to the Holy God who has helped her in her time of need; and who has equally made birth, and life, and death, and as equally vouchsafed safety in each and all? What is this that presseth in—chiefest of guests—at our marriages, in all the splendour of his yellowest glow; and waiting, with his face shrouded, with his pale lights and abounding in ghostly tapers—though in the glory of the hope of heaven!—at that last, solemn scene, where the very cause of the sable royalties—black (imperial, then, alike to poor or rich in the common spirit-threshold upon which we all stand)—is as the smallest, and very often the least thought-of, of all the show? What, to conclude, is this Fire which is so constantly about us, and of which we think so little and know so little, but which seems so overwhelmingly much? What is this wondrous, universal Element, or last proveable Soul of the World, which hath been so significantly, and yet so unsuspectedly, mythed, universally, through the intelligent ages? What is this magic reflection which is glassed through Time? We ask thinkers for an answer. But only out of their meditations—only out of the impossibility of denial—do we hope to wring the confession of the Divine Spirit that is in the Fire.

Of course, we mean not, in this, Real Fire. But a something of which the Real Fire is an image. Being the imparticled SPIRIT, in which everything is at one, as in which everything is possible. In this sense, real things (in the world) are the things only unreal. And unreal things (out of the world) are the only real.

In short, in our book, we have sought to cast loose the chains which men think they have of this dense, solid, soulless world of ours. Ignoring Spirit out of it, as a thing of no account. Rejecting miracle, because it will not submit to a machinery which produces the world. But which is, of course, incompetent to explain the masterships over itself. Which machinery dissolves wholly at the frontier that separates the great, outside, unknown world, from the little, inside, known world.

Ours is not so much an attempt to restore to Super-stition its dispossessed pedestal, as it is to replace the Supernatural upon its abdicated throne. Also to dis-cover what the nature of this FIRE should be, which seems to have been the thing earliest worshipped in the world, and continued traces of which worship survive not only over all Europe, but in our own country.

And if, after listening, for so long a time, to the mighty eloquence of Saint Paul, when heaping in-ference on inference and proof on proof concerning the religion of the Redeemer, of which he was then so triumphant a champion, Agrippa breaks up his charmed revery (in which he, himself, touches on the confine of conviction) with the astonished exclama-tion :—"Paul, Paul, thou almost persuadest me to be a Christian!" may we not hope that, now, to the re-flecting reader, such light of probability shall shine from our arguments, as that he, too, shall "almost see" that the Supernatural may be possible about him even in his own familiar hours, and in this our modern present day?

CHAPTER XXIV.

ASTRONOMY AND MIND-SCIENCE.

THE true religion ought—if from anywhere—to come from the nature around us, and to be derived from the philosophic views of it. That is, from out of that nature, rightly read. And yet such, in the modern day, is the exaggeration of the importance of science upon its own account—as if science were anything apart from the right philosophic uses of it—that nature—even by the scientific lights which are obtained out of it—is misread in most directions.

We proceed to cite the opinions of a modern and a very able (as a very comprehensively regardful) author, who has most successfully, we think, sought to diminish the confidence, and boasting, of mankind even in their astronomy. Which, in the main, is the soundest of all man's science.

We do not undervalue science. We only seek to direct it to its proper uses; and to prevent it from being taken as the explanation of things with which it has nothing in common.

We pass to make a few remarks on some points connected with the "Star-Eyed Science," premising that we do not assume much in regard of the details of the study. Our views will be found, in some important points, peculiar; and certainly in some respects, very different to those ordinarily entertained.

We yield to no man in admiration of the splendours

of the heavens. They are a book of grandeur, opened every night over our heads, and each beautiful star includes a great and living moral. But we think, first, that the terms "Infinity" and "Immensity" are unduly applied to them. Secondly, that they give us no new light as to the history or destiny of man. Thirdly, that the telescope, as a mental and magical instrument, has been overrated. Fourthly, that the inference of the insignificance of man, drawn from the vastness of the universe, is altogether illogical. Fifthly, that astronomical discovery has nearly reached its limit. Sixthly, that the *astronomy of man's soul* is infinitely grander than that of the starry heavens, and is but distantly related to it. And, finally, that there is no reason to believe that death, and the immortality which lies beyond, will allow us to remain in those material regions of which the stars seem the very bright lights.

We hope for our reader's indulgence as we try to explain more fully what we mean.

First. We hear astronomers often speaking of those " Infinities ;"—those " Immensities." These are words which, though used sometimes rhetorically, are always calculated to give a false impression to the general mind. The universe is *not* infinite. As well say of a drop of water that it is infinite, as that a universe is. The vastest and most complicated firmament is not one step nearer the abstract, and absolute, idea of Infinity, than is a curled shaving amongst the heap on the floor of a joiner's shop. The infinite aspect the Creation assumes, is a mere illusion of our eye ; the dimness of a weak and unbounded vision. The universe is just the multiplication of a sand-grain, or fire-particle. And, by multiplying the finite, how can we reach the infinite? Who can, by searching, find out God? "To an inconceivably superior being," says Coleridge, "the whole fabric of creation may appear as one plain, the distance between stars and systems seeming, to him, but as that between particles of earth to us. Say, rather, it is highly probable that this vast universe seems to God but as one distinctly rounded atom, swimming in the viewless ocean of the true Infinite." That which is higher than Heaven, deeper than Hell, and broader than wing of angel can traverse.

"A metaphysical difficulty," says Isaac Taylor, if we need enforce a statement so obvious by authority, "prevents us from ever regarding the material universe as infinite." And if not infinite, what is it but an exaggeration of any toy-bubble? Away, then, with the words which sound magnificently but mean nothing, of "infinity" and "immensity," applied to that mere framework of that which is contained within it. That framework—or that matter—is all that our earthly eyes, or telescopes, now, or ever, can possibly behold.

Secondly. Those prodigious discoveries of the Newtonian and Herschellian heavens have not really told us anything in reference to the great mystery of man; of his being, history, destiny, or relation to God. They have simply transferred and magnified the difficulties by which we are environed on this island of earth. They have not hitherto shed one beam on any moral theme. It is as yet utterly uncertain—for all the stars can teach us—whether the universe, beyond our globe, be peopled or not. On the moral

state of their populations—if populations there be—
the sky, however strictly questioned or cross-questioned,
remains obstinately silent. In fact, a multitude of
human faces, silently looking up towards an uncom-
mon appearance in the heavens, would reflect as much
light *up into it* as do the stars down upon the anomalous and awful condition of the children of men.
Blank ignorance, blind astonishment, or helpless pity,
are all the feelings with which even imagination can
invest that still, persevering, and solemn gaze. Foster,
in one of his journals, seems rather to rejoice in the
notion that the stars are of fire. Because, in this,
there is one link connecting us with the remotest
luminaries of the vast arch. Some philosophers doubt,
we believe, if this be a fact. But, at all events, we
wonder that he did not see, on his own showing, and
in accordance with his own gloomy notions, that the
universe might be literally called one vast Hell, or
burning fiery furnace, to be quenched only in the
final extinction of all things. If the stars *are* fire, it
may be a fire in which all the earths and alkalis, and
all the chemical combinations around them, are slowly
but certainly to be consumed.

And thus the great mirror of the midnight heavens
becomes rather a reflection of the austere purposes of
the Divine Destruction, than of the prosperous career
of the worlds of regenerate man. In fact, we humbly
conceive that the discovery of a new family of *animal-
culæ,* or of a new series of minerals, would cast as
much light upon human nature and human history as
the disclosure of firmament upon firmament of distant
and inscrutable flame.

Thirdly. The telescope, as a mental and magical instrument, has been overrated. The imagination of a poet, in a single dream, can immeasurably outstrip all its revelations. What has it told us, after all? It informs us that our sun, a light or glowing spark, has innumerable fellows of it dispersed through space. And that these dots of flame, by their distribution nearer or farther from each other, have assumed certain shapes: which are, however, perpetually shifting and changing. Driving, like the clouds on a windy day; and magnifying and altering form in proportion to the power of the instrument through which they are surveyed.

In truth, there are views of astronomy in Addison's "Spectator," a century old, as sublime as any that have been written since. And what have the two Herschells, or Arago, or Nicol done to answer the questions: *What* is a sun? *What* is a system? *What* is a firmament? or, *What* is the one "fiery particle" which pervades and forms, it is said, by expansion, the whole? It is as if a man, questioned as to the purpose of an umbrella, were to reply only by opening it, and deeming that thus the query was answered.

The telescope, in one word, has only widened the periphery of our view, but has not admitted us, really, into one of the secrets of the heavens. The mystery of the above has merely been transferred, unsolved, to the Star-Universe.

CHAPTER XXV.

THE ASTRONOMY OF THE MIND.

FOURTHLY. The inference of the insignificance of man, from the magnitude of the Creation, is miserably illogical. A man, in reality, is as much overcome by the size of a hill, or a house, as by that of the Herschellian skies. A mountain is a noble object. But why? Because man sees it, and sheds the glory, and the meaning, of his own soul over it. A sun is but a burnished plate till it is vivified by the same process, and man has said of it, in reverent imitation of the Demiurgic Artist, "It is very good." The stars, too, must all (so to speak) wait, in the chamber of the human comprehension, to receive their homage, to be told of their numbers, and to listen to their names. Even although these splendid bodies may be peopled, man has no evidence that those beings are greater, or of a different kind, to himself. Any more than he has evidence that snow and the fierce sunshine of the tropics, anxiety, misery, and death, are confined to his own globe. Which dark, torn, and ruptured to the near eye, is (as the author of "Festus" expresses it) "shining fair, whole, and spotless, a living well of light" to spectators in the far-off depths of the sky.

What, in fact, are the increasing, and receding, and multiplying firmaments, but as the steps of the ladder on which man is climbing every year, without ever coming nearer to his great ultimate inheritance—

P

space ; eternity ;—and God !   Poor Pascal, on the bed from which he never rose, saw the whole truth on this subject.   " The universe is not so great as I.   It might, indeed, fall and crush me.   But I would know it was crushing me ; while it would crush blindly.   I should be conscious of its destruction of me.   It would not be conscious of its extinction of me !"

Fifthly. It is clear to us that astronomical discovery has nearly reached its limit.   That God designed to it a distinct and not distant period, seems plain from the separation which is effected of other worlds from ours, by the nature of the human eye, by distance, and by that *dancing* appearance in the objects which we are told increases with the power of the telescope ; and which makes the stars, in the telescopic field, *reel like drunkards*, instead of submitting to the calm inquest of the astronomic glasses.

All our recent methods, too, of accounting for the stellar creation, such as the nebular hypothesis, have been utterly exploded.   And it is very curious how that world, the very nearest to us—the moon—seems the most perverse and inscrutable of all those heavenly puzzles.   And it seems strange to us how, having looked so long on our apparently absurd world, and particularly on the theories propounded concerning it, we have hitherto forborne to laugh.   Even with Lord Rosse's telescope to aid him, man may be seen vainly stretching, in idea, over the great air gulf :—his defeated eyes baffled because he has reached at last the limits of the possibilities of his nature.

Sixthly.   But why should we therefore repine, or sit down and weep?

Can our own soul afford no scope ! Are there no heavens within ; no firmaments of possibility of *central* and celestial light. Astronomy is, doubtless, a science the most magnificent. But the mind, itself, which has elected the telescope as our assistant for its sublime investigations, is surely as worthy of its examination— nay, is it not infinitely more so ? Incalculable are the sciences buried in the depths of the possibilities of the mind of man. Magic lieth in it, which knoweth all without science. Faith lieth in it, which can *make worlds.* What comet so wonderful as the human will ? What sun so warm and mysterious as the human heart ? What Double-Orbed gemini to be compared with the eyes of man ?—gates through which heaven shall look ! What clustered units of the stellar creation are like the wondrous mechanism of the thinking brain ; evolving its magnetism—projecting its nervous undulations even as the radiating *nebula* sends forth its thin films of suns ? What conception of a universe, however vast and complex, can be named as so astonishing as man ? —scarce a mathematical point in size, and yet spanning earth ; measuring ocean ; emptying out the clouds above him ; travelling through—by his instruments— the immortal skies, poetising, into another heaven of forms, the dust below his feet ;—in short, *worshipping God,* and sending out his ambitious thoughts into eternity. Longing, under the Almighty, for a share of it. And yet, like his progenitor Adam, while aiming perpetually to be as a God, as often losing his balance, and becoming inferior to the brute.

Why seek so eagerly to explore firmaments till we have explored the realm of our own mind ? That which lieth so open, and that so inviteth, and that, yet, is so neglected! And, alas! no light do all the lights of all the firmaments, however beautiful, however grand, however inexpressibly wondrous, however accumulated into meaning by the Godlike powers of genius :—alas, no illumination does the whole frame of creation cast upon the mystery of man's moral condition; his nature as a sinner; or the hope he has of forgiveness, and of everlasting life! For why? Man is essentially a spirit. Whereas the universe of matter is but a " fire-made," glorious, and consuming cinder!

CHAPTER XXVI.

THE SOUL AND THE STELLAR UNIVERSE.

WE take leave of this scanty view of a magnificent theme by uttering, Seventhly, what may appear our most paradoxical assertion.

Namely, that there is no reason to believe that death, and immortality, will permit the emancipated soul to remain amid those present starry splendours. However bright, and even, at times, inviting they seem, they contain no home for us after we are freed from these tabernacles of clay. We often hear men talking as if, somehow, their heaven lay in the upper space, as if, in a manner of which they can give us no idea—which they cannot even render distinct to their own minds—they went up, after death, as "forms" among the heavenly bodies.

It were wrong in us to dogmatise on any such sacred question. But it seems more probable, and more scriptural, too, that we pass, at death, amid a purely spiritual scenery, as well as into a purely spiritual state. Or, at least, that the lower *phenomena* of matter will be, then, as invisible to us as are, doubtless, now, the immaterial worlds. This conviction came upon us, years ago, with a sudden and startling force, which we felt more than enough for our own mind. Taking up, shortly after, one of the strange reveries of poor misdirected Edgar Poe, we were surprised to find the following: "At death, these creatures, enjoying the ultimate life—immortality ; act all things, and pass everywhere by mere volition—indwelling not the stars, which to us seem the sole palpabilities, and for the filling with which we blindly deem space created—*but that space, itself;*—that infinity, of which the true substantive vastness swallows up the *star shadows*—blotting them out from the perception of the angels." And again, " the stars, through what we consider their materiality, escape the angelic sense, just as the unparticled matter, or space, through what we consider its immateriality, eludes the perception of organic and incarnate beings."

Inferences of much interest might be drawn from these cursory remarks. We might gather, for instance, that there was, and is, no alternative for man—but Revelation or despair. Nature can, at the utmost, do little for us. It can tell us very little. This, the highest of philosophers have ever felt (including some of the Alchemists). And, hence, they have tried to get *behind nature :*—and to get so behind it, as to read the future of the past. In reading rightly—that is, out of their own nature—they have all miserably failed. And ever shall they so fail. One only reached the ultimate secrets of this sublime and mysterious scheme of things. One only—living—was permitted to pass behind the tremendous veil of creation. And why? Because he came from the excellent Glory (which is, perhaps, only another name for that "unparticled matter," that sublime Reality of existence which is within all things) ; as well as because he confirmed his power by privilege of virtue. He, alone, even in the days of his flesh, with unveiled face looked upon the Glory of God.

And this power he gives, already, in some measure, and shall yet more fully bestow upon his faithful, and great-hearted, but humblest-minded followers:—that they, too, shall behold, in the living and illuminated depths of their own mind, as in a glass—more glorious than in the mirror of the unnumbered stars—more glorious than in the face of the whole creation—the inexpressible greatness—the inexhaustible pity for us, of the Lord God, the Creator and Protector of us all!

Once more, how overwhelmingly grand the views opened to us by such thoughts as these! Here, indeed, are "new heavens and a new earth!" Here, in every death, is the transacting, beforehand, of that tremendous scene in which the heavens are to flee away. The sight of those beautiful, yet terrible and tantalising starry heavens, are, at every death-view, exchanged for the prospect of the spiritual *empyrean;* whose light is that of the soul, and whose life is indeed life! Immortal splendours to which even the sun shall be as the blackness of death itself. Heaven-scenery which "no eye hath seen." Angelic harmonies which "no ear hath heard." These shall be for the believer. These shall be for the pure liver.

That material universe which was as the soil out of which the lucid flowers—as souls—should be raised, dissolves like a sun-penetrated clod. And the chosen spirit is rescued withinside the barrier of the unseen, and beholds matter *as it is;* space *as it is;* God *as he is!* It knoweth, now, what is the meaning of the words:—"the light *inaccessible* and full of glory." Nor will the soul, thus motived with immaterial light, miss the strange and coarse world-materials which blackened its birth.

There is much in the world on which he lives, as well as in the worlds of stars, that is beautiful to man. But there is much also that is perplexing, sad; nay, fearful. But here, over this Spirit Land, the sun of truth shines full, and never changes his glory. *That* world hath no need of the material sun, nor of the moon to light it up. The Being that is transferred to it, has only to look up, and to see, without cloud, or shadow, or reflected shining, Knowledge; Truth; Eternity;—God! It shall look back upon the stars as but bright toys. It shall regard them as things which—for it—have passed into dust.

Further we dare not penetrate. Here shall we cease. But—ceasing—shall we not end with the solemn words of the only Book which has given us authentic and commanding tidings from those unknown worlds? "Seeing, therefore, that all these things shall be dissolved, what should ye not make yourselves as heirs of this heaven?" This heaven into which all—in the final glory—shall be absorbed.

CHAPTER XXVII.

CLOSE OF THE ARGUMENT.

WE have done. We have presented the reader with philosophical results. Thirty-nine years of metaphysics are exhibited in the conclusions of this book. They have, thus, the guarantee of delay and of thought. Much thinking produces the firmest convictions.

We have had no desire to parade the learned machinery, through the laborious application of which, the sparks of truth are elicited. Nothing could have been easier—if we had followed the usual modern philosopher's practice—than fortifying—or, as we may say, *stiffening* our pages with endless reference; with ever-thickening quotations; deluging our disquisitions with learned material, bristling with Greek, Hindostanee, Hebrew, and what not! We could have displayed—had we so chosen—the interior of our workshop. For there is the learned workshop, as well as that of the mechanic. And in an ostentatious exhibition of the lists, we might, indeed, have totally lost sight—doubtless, we should have lost sight—of the grand purpose to which we sought to apply them.

Rather than to the never-ending array of philosophical *furniture;* of all times, of all countries, and the work of many men's hands—some of whom are very masters in their craft; but in which number are also others who are mere system-mongers:—rather than this, have we sought to point to the stable chair —made by ourselves, as it were, out of the wood of others—in which the enquirer shall the most safely be able to sit himself down. Or to try, at least, himself so to do. We are weary of jargon. We are harassed, out of all life of endurance, with religious contention. We think that, of many books, the very best part of them is their outside. We know that languages, whether understood or not, are the easiest things in the world out of which to make a show; and that citations of reverend and philosophic authors, whether apposite or only thought so (between which there lieth great difference), are most readily furnished. There are libraries and there are pens and ink; of both of which to make use.

Anything can be said for anything. The very oldest philosophies, the very immutable truths, are now-a-days made successful use of as personal advertisement. Aware that thus it is in many respects, we have carefully—and with an exceeding hatred of the display of it—avoided that which is called *learning*.

But amidst all the curious stores and learned tomes in the very plenitude of which the explorer's attention has been distracted as in a mine, there is a group of books—and especially one book—which we must notice as presenting an almost incredible body of knowledge. As a prince in this noble cluster, stands: —"*Anacalypsis;* or, an Inquiry into the Origin of Languages, Nations, and Religions. By Godfrey Higgins, Esq., F.S.A., F.R. Asiat. Soc., F.R. Ast. Soc.; of Skelton Grange, near Doncaster. Two vols., quarto. London: Longman, Rees, Orme, Brown, Green, and Longman, Paternoster Row, 1836." We did not discover this book until, by the mere force of hard thinking, we had achieved to its truths, and, by analogical study, had struck out already, as a system for ourself, its leading ideas. In it, however, we were delighted to find all the wealth of sagacity, of particulars, and of detail, which raise the astonishing, ancient, occult system, of which we are the disciple, into law. This noble work of the distinguished man, the Author of the "*Anacalypsis*," was the conquest of twenty years, of ten hours per day, as he, himself, confesses. The other books, though, in a manner, thoroughly unconscious even to the producers of them—which contain the historical outline of the grand secret system of Rosicrucianism, are—" The Celtic Druids; or, an Attempt to show that the Druids were the Priests of Oriental Colonies, who emigrated to India, and were the Introducers of the first, or Cadmæan, System of Letters, and the builders of Stonehenge, Carnac, and of other Cyclopean Works in Asia and Europe. By Godfrey Higgins, Esq. London: Rowland Hunter, St. Paul's Churchyard, and Ridgway and Sons, Piccadilly, 1829." "The Round Towers of Ireland. An Illustrated Treatise, published by the Royal Irish Academy, on the Origin, Purpose, and Character of the famous Round Towers of Ireland. With a Dissertation on the Mysteries of Freemasonry, Sabæism, and of Buddhism. By Henry O'Brien. One volume, 8vo, 1834." "The *Œdipus Judaicus*. By the Right Hon. Sir William Drummond. London, printed by A. J. Valpy, 1811." And an

"Essay on a Punic Inscription, including a variety of Biblical Criticism." By the same author.

A farther show of multitudinous books—and the especial hard use we have made of them—all this necessary to the perfecting of the deductions which we draw, would have helped no result. It would only have served to surprise. Every reader is infinitely more concerned in that which you tell, than in your methods of the acquisition of it. He is not desirous to be made acquainted with the laborious means through which you may have been enabled to inform him of something. The watch to mark his time is that which the customer asks. He wants not a recapitulation of the multitudinous and perplexing science through which, by good fortune, and by hard study, you stand there prepared to place it ready for use in his hand. Greek, Latin, and Hebrew quotations, *pro* and *con.*, and learned words, are as the gold and silver filings, the motive powers, cogs, and *disjecta membra*, the odds and ends of the watchmaker's machinery. Such are better kept out of sight ; such are better removed with the artificer's apron, than paraded as a ground for admiration, and as a challenge to wonder. This is absurd and out of taste when, in the philosopher's great clock-making shop, bells should strike responsive, if possible, to the immortal leading-chimes : and when the prodigious Seconds of Time should be told as Great Nature (and nature alone) sets herself the eternal hands !

To the guardians of the more recondite and secret philosophical knowledge, of whom, in the societies—abroad and at home—there are a greater number, even in these days, than the uninitiate might suppose, it will be sufficient to observe that in no part of our Book (though every reader will find—we presume—abundance of entertainment in it) is there approach, by us, to disclosures which, in any mind, might be considered too little guarded.

And now we take leave of our momentous subject. We end it with the utmost humility—with inexpressible self-abasement! Fearfully do we cease with sublimities which shall overtax men's comprehension. And, as fellow-travellers through this, as yet Unnamed Waste; and as brother pilgrims through the shadows —feeling as the child shall feel, in his unutterable solitude in the encircling shades of the blackening forest when the daylight fails—cheered by the hope, alone, of the mercy of that Divine Father of us all "which art in Heaven," and of whom it is said, that "even not a sparrow shall fall to the ground without his benevolent cognisance of the little death:" —in this fearing and reliant faith do we exchange farewells with the reader.

APPENDIX A.

HISTORY OF THE MAGI.

OUR exposition of the Occult Philosophy, regarding which we have sought to supply clearer ideas to the attentive reader, would be incomplete and would, we think, lack dignity, if we were not to furnish a brief historical account, gathered up from most valuable sources, not only of the Magi, but also of the singular, ancient, mysterious race or tribe of the primeval Cabiri. Traces of the strange worship of whom, and tokens of whose transcendental legends, are in all countries (as observable through all history)—to be encountered.

The Magi may be described, in a word, as the high priests of ancient Persia, and the profound cultivators of the wisdom of Zoroaster. They were instituted by Cyrus when he founded the new Persian empire, and are supposed to have been of the Median race. Schlegel says ("Philosophy of History," Lecture vii), "They were not so much an hereditary sacerdotal caste, as an order or association, divided into various and successive ranks and grades, such as existed in the mysteries—the grade of apprenticeship—that of mastership—that of perfect mastership." In short, they were a theosophical college; and either its professors were called indifferently "magi," or magicians, and "wise men," or they were distinguished into two classes by those names.

" The Magi," says the author of ZOROASTER, in the quarto edition of the "Encyclopædia Metropolitana," "were the priests and philosophers of the ancient Persians, distinguished not only for their knowledge of theology, but also for their intimate acquaintance with the secrets of nature.

> "'Ille penes Persas *Magus* est qui sidera novit,
>   Qui sciat herbarum vires, cultumque deorum.'"

Their name pronounced 'Mogh' by the modern* Persians, and 'Magh' by the ancients (Jer. xxxix. 3, 13), signified 'Wise, as appears from Daniel, v. 2, compared with Jeremiah xxxix. 3 ; and such is the interpretation of it given by the Greek and Roman writers. (Hesychius, v. Μάγος, Apuleius, 'Apol.' i., Porphyr. 'de Abstinentiâ,' iv., fol. 92.) ·Stobæus (p. 496) expressly calls the science of the Magi (ἡμαγεια) the service of the gods (θεῶν θεραπεία); so Plato ('in Alcib.' 1.) [According to Ennemoser, "Maginsiah, Madschusie, signified the office and knowledge of the priest, who was called 'Mag,' 'Magius,' 'Magiusi,' and afterwards 'Magi' and 'Magician.' Brucker maintains ('Historia Philosophica Critica,' i. 160) that the primitive meaning of the word is 'fire-worshipper,' 'worship of the light,' to which erroneous opinion he has been led by the Mahommedan dictionaries. In the modern Persian the word is "Mog,' and 'Mogbed' signifies high priest. The high priest of the Parsees, at Surat, even at the present day, is called 'Mobed.' Others derive the word from 'Megh;' 'Meh-ab' signifying something which is great

---

* The Vedas describe the Persian religion to have come from Upper India.

and noble, and Zoroaster's disciples were called 'Meghestom.'" ('Reference to Kleuker and Wachsmuth.') Salverte states that these Mobeds are still named in the Pehivi dialect 'Magoi.'] They were divided into three classes:—1. Those who abstained from all animal food. 2. Those who never ate of the flesh of any tame animals: and, 3. Those who made no scruple to eat any kind of meat. A belief in the transmigration of the soul was the foundation of this abstinence. They professed the science of divination, and for that purpose met together and consulted in their temples. ('Cic. de Div.,' 99.) They professed to make truth the great object of their study; for that alone, they said, can make man like God (Oromazes), "whose body resembles light, as his soul or spirit resembles truth." (Porphyr 'in vitâ Pythagoræ,' p. 185.) They condemned all images, and those who said that the gods are male and female (Diogen. Laertius); they had neither temples nor altars, but worshipped the sky, as a representative of the Deity, on the tops of mountains: they also sacrificed to the sun, moon, earth, fire, water, and winds, says Herodotus (1. 25); meaning, no doubt, that they adored the heavenly bodies and the elements. This was probably before the time of Zoroaster, when the religion of Persia seems to have resembled that of ancient India. Their hymns in praise of the Most High exceeded, according to Dio Chrysostom ('Orat. Borysthen,' 36), the sublimity of anything in Homer or Hesiod. They exposed their dead bodies to wild beasts. (Cicero, loc. cit.)" His reference is to Thomas Hyde's 'Historia Religionis veterum Persarum;'

and to Kleuker, 'Anhang zum Zendavesta,' Leip.,
1783.

Schlegel also continues, that it is a question
"whether the old Persian doctrine and 'Lichtsage'
(wisdom or tradition of light) did not undergo material alterations in the hands of its Median restorer,
Zoroaster; or whether this doctrine was preserved, in
all its purity, by the order of the Magi." He then
remarks, that on them devolved the important trust
of the monarch's education, which must necessarily
have given them great weight and influence in the
State. "They were in high credit at the 'Persian
gates'—for that was the Oriental name given to the
capital of the empire, and the abode of the prince—
and they took the most active part in all the factions
that encompassed the throne, or were formed in the
vicinity of the court. In Greece, and even in Egypt,
the sacerdotal fraternities and associations of initiates,
formed by the mysteries, had in general but an indi-
rect, though not unimportant, influence on affairs of
State; but in the Persian monarchy they acquired a
complete political ascendency." This is only so far
of moment to our present subject as it leads to the
remark that the whole ancient world was in reality
governed by the Magi, either openly or in secret; and
that the reason of their so great power was the high
wisdom they cultivated. Religion, philosophy, and
the sciences were all in their hands; they were the
universal physicians who healed the sick in body and
in spirit, and, in strict consistency with that character,
ministered to the State, which is only the man again
in a larger sense.

The three grades of the Magi alluded to in the passage cited above, and from Schlegel, are called by Herder ("Mobed et Destur-Mobed"), the "disciples," the "professed," and the "masters." They were originally from Bactria, where they governed a little state by laws of their own choice, and by their incorporation in the Persian Empire they greatly promoted the consolidation of the conquests of Cyrus. Their fall dates from the reign of Darius Hystaspes, about 500 B.C., by whom they were fiercely persecuted; this produced an emigration which extended to Cappadocia on the one hand, and to India on the other, but they were still of so much consideration at a later period as to provoke the jealousy of Alexander the Great. It is, in all probability, to the emigration of the Magi that we must attribute the spread of magic in Greece and Arabia.*

So much critical acumen and mystical research has been expended on the subject of the *Cabiri* and the ancient mysteries, and it is so intimately connected with the origin of all mythology, and with the ancient creeds of philosophy and religion, that we can attempt little more than a bare indication of its nature. The

---

* "The mysteries celebrated within the recesses of the *hypogea* (caverns, or labyrinths) were precisely of that character which are called Free-Masonic, or Cabiric. The signification of this latter epithet is, as to written letters, a desideratum. Selden has missed it; so has Origen, and Sophocles. Strabo, too, and Montfaucon, have been equally astray. Hyde was the only one who had any *idea* of its *composition*, when he declared "It was a *Persian word*, somewhat altered from *Gabri*, or *Guebri*, and signifying Fire-Worshippers." — O'Brien's "Round Towers of Ireland," p. 354.

Cabiri are often mentioned as powerful magicians, but more generally as the most ancient gods of whose worship there is any record, while their mysteries, called Samothracian, designate the form in which that worship, and the philosophy in which it was grounded, are recognised by antiquaries. The mysteries of Eleusis and Bacchus are of recent date compared with these antique rites; which, in fact, are lost in antiquity,* and extend far beyond the historical period. The facts as stated by Noël, in his very valuable "Dictionnaire de la Fable," 1823, 4th ed., are briefly these :—

Phericydes, Herodotus, and Nonnus, speak of the Cabiri as sons of Vulcan, which is the opinion adopted

---

* Brutus, grandson of Æneas, having killed his father Sylvius, fled from Italy; and after joining himself to some emigrants from Troy in Greece, and undergoing many adventures, he landed at Tot-ness in Devonshire. The island was inhabited by "giants;" he conquered them, and seized the island. He had three sons; Locrin or Locgrin, to whom he gave Loegria, that is, England; Camber, to whom he gave Wales, hence called "Cambria;" and Albanact, to whom he gave Scotland, which from him was called "Albania." Here we have the old Mythos:—the going-out, the adventurous journey, and the Father, Brutus, and Three Sons, like Adam and Cain, Abel and Seth; or Noah and Shem, Ham, and Japhet. This history is found in Geoffrey of Monmouth, and is now always regarded as a fiction of the Monks of the Middle Ages. But the single fact of the game "Troy," in Wales, being noticed by Pliny, joined to the names of the countries, raises a strong probability that Geoffrey did but repeat the tradition which he found. "Tot-ness" is "Tat-ness," or "nase," or town of the promontory of "Tat," "Taranus," or *Buddha*. It stands very near a remarkable peninsula or promontary. See "*Anacalypsis.*" "Ness" is rather "naze," "noss," "nose," or cape or promontory headland or point or projection. "Naso"—Latin—nose.

by Fabretti. Cicero calls them sons of Proserpine; and Jupiter is often named as their father, which Noël thinks may be the reason of their identification with Castor and Pollux, known as the Dioscuri. Dionysius of Halicarnassus, Macrobius, Varro, and others, consider them the same as the Penates of the Romans; in which, however, the Venetian Altori is opposed to them. According to his opinion, and that of Vossius, the Cabiri were nothing more than the ministers of the gods, who were deified after their death; and the Dactyli, the Curetes, and the Corybantes, were only other names by which they were known. Strabo regards them as the ministers of Hecate. Bochart, in fine, recognises in them the three principal infernal deities, Pluto, Proserpine, and Mercury. Such are the conflicting opinions recorded by Noël, which, as we shall presently see, have been regulated somewhat by a more recent author, Mr. Kenrick. The worship of the Cabiri, if the general belief is to be credited, was originally derived from Egypt, where we find the ancient temple of Memphis consecrated to them. Herodotus supposes that the Pelasgians, the first inhabitants of the Peloponnesus, dwelt first in the isle of Samothrace, where they introduced this worship, and established the famous mysteries, into which such heroes as Cadmus, Orpheus, Hercules, Castor, Pollux, Ulysses, Agamemnon, Æneas, and Philip, the father of Alexander, had the honour of being initiated. From their abode in Samothrace, the Pelasgi carried these mysteries to Athens; whence they were conveyed to Thebes. Æneas, after the ruin of his country, in like manner introduced the worship of the Cabiri into Italy, his new home; and there they were invoked in all cases of domestic misfortune, and became the household gods of the people.

We shall notice, before concluding, the theory of Pococke, who has undertaken to divest these ancient traditions of all mystery. Here it is proper to remark that the name of the Cabiri is generally derived from the Phœnician, signifying powerful gods, and both the Latins and Greeks called them " Dii Potentes," or " Dii Socii," associated gods. It is probable the *esoteric*, or real name, was only revealed to initiates. The ancient figures, representing them, generally convey the idea of power or warlike energy, by a dart, a lance, or a hammer. Here the conclusions of Mr. Kenrick, as we gather them from a somewhat extended criticism in his " Egypt before Herodotus," may be briefly represented as follows :—

1. The existence of the worship of the Cabiri, at Memphis, under a pigmy form, and its connection with the worship of Vulcan. The coins of Thessalonica also establish this connection; those which bear the legend " Kabeiros" having a figure with a hammer in his hand, the *pileus* and apron of Vulcan, and sometimes an anvil near the feet.

2. The Cabiri belonged also to the Phœnician Theology. The proofs are drawn from the state-ments of Herodotus. Also the coins of Cossyra, a Phœnician settlement, exhibit a dwarfish figure with the hammer and short apron, and sometimes a radiated head, apparently allusive to the element of fire, like the star of the Dioscuri.

3. The isle of Lemnos was another remarkable seat

of the worship of the Cabiri and of Vulcan, as representing the element of fire. Mystic rites were celebrated here, over which they presided, and the coins of the island exhibit the head of Vulcan, or a Cabirus, with the *pileus*, hammer, and forceps. It was this connection with fire, metallurgy, and the most remarkable product of the art in weapons of war, which caused the Cabiri to be identified with the Cureks of Etolia, the Idæi Dactyli of Crete, the Corybantes of Phrygia, and the Telchines of Rhodes. They were the same probably in Phœnician origin, the same in mystical and orgiastic rites, but different in number, genealogy, and local circumstances, and by the mixture of other mythical traditions, according to the various countries in which their worship prevailed. The fable that one Cabirus had been killed by his brother, or brothers, was probably a moral *mythos*, representing the result of the invention of armour, and analogous to the story of the mutual destruction of the men in brazen armour, who sprang from the dragon's teeth sown by Cadmus and Jason. It is remarkable that the name of the first fratricide signifies a " lance," and in Arabic a " smith."

4. The worship of the Cabiri prevailed, also, in Imbros, near the entrance of the Hellespont, which makes it probable that the great gods, in the neighbouring island of Samothrace, were of the same origin. The Cabiri, Curetes, and Corybantes, appear to have represented air as well as fire. This island was inhabited by Pelasgi, who may have derived their worship from the Phœnicians, and who, now, mingled it with dogmas and ceremonies derived from

the neighbouring country of Thrace and Phrygia, and with the old Pelasgic mysteries of Ceres. Hence the various explanations given of the Samothracian deities, and the number of them, so differently stated; some making them two, some four, some eight; the latter agreeing with the number of early Egyptian deities mentioned by Herodotus. It is still probable that their number was two, from their identification with the Dioscuri and Tyndaridæ, and from the number of the Patæci on Phœnician vessels. The addition of Vulcan, as their father, or brother, made them three; and a fourth may have been their mother, Cabira.

5. The Samothracian divinities continued to be held in high veneration in late times, but are commonly spoken of in connection with navigation, as the twin Dioscuri, or Tyndaridæ; on the other hand, the Dioscuri are spoken of as the Curetes, or Corybantes. The coins of Tripolis exhibit the spears and star of the Dioscuri, with the legend " Cabiri."

6. The Roman Penates have been identified with the Dioscuri, and Dionysius states that he had seen two figures, of ancient workmanship, representing youths, armed with spears, which, from an antique inscription on them, he knew to be meant for Penates. So, the " Lares" of Etruria and Rome.

7. The worship of the Cabiri furnishes the Key to the wanderings of Æneas, the foundation of Rome, and the War of Troy itself, as well as the Argonautic expedition. Samothrace and the Troad were so closely connected with this worship, that it is difficult to judge in which of the two it originated; and the

Gods of Lavinium, the supposed colony from Troy, were Samothracian, also the Palladium, a pigmy image, was connected at once with Æneas and the Troad, with Rome, Vesta, and the Penates, and the religious belief and traditions of several towns in the south of Italy. Mr. Kenrick also recognises a mythical personage in Æneas, whose attributes were derived from those of the Cabiri, and continues with some interesting observations on the Homeric fables. He concludes that the essential part of the War of Troy originated in the desire to connect together, and explain, the traces of an ancient religion. In fine, he notes one other remarkable circumstance, that the countries in which the Samothracian and Cabiriac worship prevailed were peopled either by the Pelasgi or by the Æolians, who, of all the tribes comprehended under the general name Hellenes, approach the most nearly, in antiquity and language, to the Pelasgi. " We seem warranted, then" (our author observes), " in two conclusions: first, that the Pelasgian tribes in Italy, Greece, and Asia were united, in times reaching high above the commencement of history, by community of religious ideas and rites, as well as letters, arts, and language ; and secondly, that large portions of what is called the heroic history of Greece, are nothing else than fictions devised to account for the traces of this affinity, when time, and the ascendency of other nations, had destroyed the primitive connection, and rendered the cause of the similarity obscure. The original derivation of the Cabiriac system from Phœnicia and Egypt is a less certain, though still highly probable conclusion.

8. The name "Cabiri" has been very generally deduced from the Phœnician "mighty;" and this etymology is in accordance with the fact that the gods of Samothrace were called "Dii potentes."* Mr. Kenrick believes, however, that the Phœnicians used some other name, which the Greeks translated "Kabeiros," and that it denoted the two elements of "fire" and "wind."

These points bring the floating traditions collected by Noël and other compilers into something like order; they likewise support our belief in a primitive revelation, the history of which was symbolically represented, either by real or fictitious persons, as most convenient, in the Homeric poems, and other remains of antiquity. Mr. Pococke, however ("India in Greece," 1852), seems to reason differently; though it would be easy to convert his argument in favour of our hypothesis. "The 'Cabeiri,'" he says, "are the *Khyberi*, or people of the 'Khyber;' the 'Corybantes' are the 'Gour-boud-des,' or people of 'Ghor-bund-land,' all of whom are ' Pat-aikoi,' or Lunar tribes, that is, *Bud'hists.*" We cannot pretend to represent either the extent of Mr. Pococke's argument, or the learning with which he pursues it; but it must be evident that the transference of names from one region to another, and the proof that Palestine and Greece were colonised from India, would not affect the

---

* From the name of the Temple, now Stonehenge, comes the name of Ambresbury, abbreviated into Amesbury, which stands a few miles from it. This is called the "Ambres of the Abiri." It is two words, and means the "Ambres of the Dii potentes," or of the אבידי, or "Cabiri," for they are all the same.

radical value of those names, or the mystical import of the original symbols. So much it seems necessary to state, because the author we allude to supposes *all the mystery must necessarily disappear* from this subject when he has pointed out that the "Dii Potes" of the Greeks and Romans are simply the "Dii Bodhes," or Budha gods of Hindostan. On the contrary, we are persuaded that, whatever new light may be thrown upon these ancient systems of worship, or on the settlements of the primeval nations, it will only bring out in stronger relief the great fact, that a community of religious ideas and rites, as well as of letters, arts, and language, really existed, in times reaching high above the commencement of history, as affirmed by Mr. Kenrick. This opinion also gathers strength from the German writers cited by Ennemoser, chiefly Schweigger, who resolve the Cabiriac symbols into a system of natural philosophy, founded on the knowledge of electricity and magnetism. It would lead us too far to consider these interesting developments.

In the generations of Sanconiathon, the Cabiri are claimed for the Phœnicians, though we understand the whole mystically. The line proceeds thus :—Of the Wind and the Night were born two mortal men, Æon and Protogonus. The immediate descendants of these were " Genus" (perhaps Cain) and Genea. To Genus were born three mortal children, Phôs, Pûr, and Phlox, who discovered fire ; and these, again, begat sons of vast bulk and height, whose names were given to the mountains in which they dwelt, Cassius, Libanus, Antilibanus, and Brathu. The issue of these giant men, by their own mothers, were Meinrumus,

Hypsuranius, and Usous. Hypsuranius inhabited Tyre; and Usous, becoming a huntsman, consecrated two pillars to fire and the wind, with the blood of the wild beasts that he captured. In times long subsequent to these, the race of Hypsuranius gave being to Hagreus and Halieus, inventors, it is said, of the arts of hunting and fishing. From these descended two brothers, one of whom was Chrysor or Hephæstus (perhaps Tubal-Cain or Vulcan): this Hephæstus exercised himself in words, charms, and divinations; he also invented boats, and was the first that sailed. His brother first built walls with bricks, and their descendants, in the second generation, seem to have completed the invention of houses, by the addition of courts, porticos, and crypts. They are called Aletæ and Titans, and in their time began husbandry and hunting with dogs. From the Titans descended Amynus (perhaps Ham), and Magus, who taught men to construct villages and tend flocks; and of these two were begotten Misor (perhaps Mizraim), whose name signifies Well-freed, and Sydic, whose name denotes the Just: these found out the use of salt. We now come to the important point in this line of wonders. From Misor descended Taautus (Thoth, Athothis, or Hermes-Trismegistus), who invented letters; and from Sydic descended the Dioscuri, or Cabiri, or Corybantes, or Samothraces. These, according to Sanconiathon, first built a complete ship, and others descended from them who discovered medicines and charms. All this dates prior to Babylon and the gods of Paganism, the elder of whom are next introduced in the "Generations." Finally, Sanconiathon settles Poseidon (Neptune) and the Cabiri at Berytus; but not till circumcision, the sacrifice of human beings and the pourtrayal of the gods, had been introduced. In recording this event, the Cabiri are called husbandmen and fishermen, which leads to the presumption that the people who worshipped those ancient gods were at length called by their name. After all that has been written, perhaps the symbol of Vulcan and the Cabiri may be studied with most effect in the Mosaic Scriptures. Among the Harleian MSS. is a copy of the constitution of an ancient body of Freemasons, prefaced by a short history, commencing as follows :—" If you ask mee how this science was first invented, my answer is this. That, before the general Deluge, which is commonly called Noah's flood, there was a man called Lemeck, as you may read in the 4th of Genesis, whoe had twoe wives; the one called Adah, the other Zilla: by Adah hee begot twoe sones, Jabell and Juball; by Zilla hee had a sonne called Tuball and a daughter named Naahmah; these fower children found ye beginning of all ye craft in the world. Jabell found out geometry, and hee divided flocks of sheep and lands; hee first built a house of stone and timber. Juball found out musick. Tuball found out the smyth's trade, or craft; alsoe of gold, silver, copper, iron, and steele, &c." (MS. 1942). This Tubal, or Tubalcain, we may pretty safely identify with Vulcan, the symbol of material art, or of the man understanding and working in nature. It is only in the interpretation of this symbol, and its connection in Genesis, that we can ever hope to discover the beginning of the ancient mysteries, and of that system

of religion and philosophy that overspread Asia and
Greece. In working such a problem, the births of
these " fower children" must be looked at as so many
successive manifestations of the spirit in man, producing, in fine, the Greek understanding, and the
magic of Samothrace and Thessalonica, Naahmah, the
last born, is the Virgin Wisdom, that is, deepest in
human understanding. And hence the mystic
prophecy that Tubalcain, in the last days (Millenium),
shall find his sister Naahmah, who shall come to him
in golden attire.

The mysteries of Cabiriac worship were celebrated
at Thebes and Lemnos, but especially in the Isle of
Samothrace : the time chosen was night. The can-
didate for initiation was crowned with a garland of
olive, and wore a *purple* band round his loins. Thus
attired, and prepared by secret ceremonies (probably
mesmeric), he was seated on a throne, brilliantly
lighted, and the other initiates then danced round him
in symbolic measures. It may be imagined that
solemnities of this nature would easily degenerate into
orgies of the most immoral tendency, as the ancient
faith, and reverence for sacred things, perished ; and
such was really the case. Still, the primitive institution was pure in form and beautiful in its mystic
signification, which passed, from one ritual to another,
till its last glimmer expired in the freemasonry of a
very recent period. The general idea represented was
the passage, through death, to a higher life ; and while
the outward senses were held in the thrall of magnetism
it is probable that revelations, good or evil, were made
to the high priests of these ceremonies. The con-

nection of magical power with the traditions of the Cabiri will thus become easy of comprehension; and it is singular, as showing the same disposition in human nature, at a far distant period, that the highest degree of illumination in the secret societies of the " Illuminati" (Rosicrucians), at the period of the French Revolution, took its name from Clairvoyance.

APPENDIX B.

THE ROSICRUCIANS.

RESPECTING the real meaning and purpose of the extraordinary philosophy of the Rosicrucians, there is the profoundest general ignorance. All that is supposed of them is, that they were a mighty sect, whose acquirements—and, indeed, practice—were involved in so much mystery that the comprehension of them was scarcely possible. And this famous secret society has been not only the problem, but the amusement, and converted into the romance, of modern times. On the principle—usually a very true one—that all of the unknown must, therefore, be imposing, the story of these Cabalists has served the turn of those who sought to impress. If modern writers have made use of their history, it has been to weave up the materials into romance. The name of the Rosicrucians has been a word of might with charlatans:—they have been the means of exciting, with the dealers in fiction. The character of the mystic Fraternity—its designs and objects—have been a potent charm with all those who thought that they possessed, through it, a power of stimulating curiosity. Members of the Society of the Rosy Cross have been introduced, as heroes, in novels; —have mysteriously flitted, as the *deus ex machinâ*, through tales of the imagination. From want of knowledge of what they were, they have been supposed everything. They have been wondered at—laughed at—

feared—set down as magicians, and as exempted from the common lot of the children of men. Fanaticism, dreaming, imposture—and, in the milder form of accusation, self-delusion: all this has been assumed of them. From the curious forms in which they chose to invest their knowledge; because of the singular fables which they elected as the medium in which their secrets should be hidden, they have been looked upon as quite of another race—as scarcely men. But they have been much mistaken.

Justice is so late of arrival to all original thinkers—the terms of prejudice, and of astonishment (not in the good sense), are so long in falling off from profound researches—that, even now, the Rosicrucians—in other words, the Paracelsians or Magnetists—are totally ignored as the arch-chemists, to whose deep thoughts, and unrelaxing labours, modern science is indebted for most of its truths. As astrology (not the juggles of the stars, but the true exploration, seeking the method of being, and of working, of the glittering habitants of space):—as astrology was the mother of astronomy, so is the lore of the Hermetic Brethren (miscalled in only one of their names—and that the popular—Rosicrucians)—the groundwork of all present philosophy. On its applied side, Rosicrucianism is the very science which is so familiar and so valuable. But as the Hermetic Beliefs are a great religion, they, of course, have their popular adaptation; and, in consequence, there is a mythology to them. There must always be a machinery to every faith, through which it may be known; and the mistake of people is in accepting the childish machinery and the coarse (but

R

fitly) coloured mythology of a religion for the religion
itself, and all of it. Hence the Rosicrucians' supposed
doctrine of the invisible children of the various elements;—its sylphs or sylphids, its cobolds, crolls,
gnomes, kelps, or kelpies, its salamanders and salaman-
drines, and its ondines : hence all the picturesque but
necessary catalogue of paraded items of belief, to constitute it a system that the vulgar might accept as
reconcilable with sense. It is surprising that brighter
intelligences have not perceived all this as only cover-
ing and concealment. It ought to be seen, at once,
that it is not possible to display certain things. Mystics
are the chief priests of every religion. For perhaps
there never was a worse-founded supposition than that
knowledge was for all people. The minds of some
classes of individuals never grow. Men who have
arrived at the best of their mental possibilities, are as
much children to the higher intelligences, and are as
unfit for their knowledge (which has, however, the
great merit of being *sure to be disbelieved*), as the
children, knowledge to whom, of higher things
than their capacity admits of, we conceal and falsify
in nursery-talk. All that has, as yet, been disclosed of
the beliefs of the Rosicrucians, is fable fitted only to
the comprehension of those who demanded a *mythos*
as the first necessary of a faith. As more and more of
the light is kindled in the mind, so is the disciple
introduced into the greater and greater truth. As he,
himself, becomes fit, so are things fitted to him. And
in the mystic sense (and, because it is mystic, the only
true sense), when men leave their settled facts, and
move towards things assumed as unbelievable, they

only, by an inverse process, as it were, approach the real facts and leave their children's stories and fables. Mystical, fantastical, and transcendental—nay, impossible—as the studies and objects of the Rosicrucians seem in these modern, ultra-practical days, it is forgotten that the truths of contemporaneous science are all based on the dreams of the old thinkers. Out of natural philosophy, the occult brethren sought the spirits of natural philosophy, and to this inner heaven— so unlike ordinary life—through purifications, through invocations, through humbling and prayers, through penances to break the terms of body with the world, through fumigations and incensing to raise up another world about them, and to place themselves *en rapport* with the inhabitants of it, through the suspension of the senses, and thereby to the opening of other senses— to the shutting-out of one state, in order to the passing into another state :—to all this the Rosicrucians sought to reach.

CONCLUSION.

Is all chance? Cannot the future ever be fore-seen? Are all the strange matters told us mere fables or inventions? Are all these things the forgery of the imaginative mind, or the inverted—the self-belief of the deluded? The future is the "recorded past" to a mind conceiving all.

Whence came that fear which has always pervaded the world? How comes it that, in all times, things transcendent of the world have always been believed? Cannot history, cannot science (worthless before these subjects; consequently useless before the truest interests of mankind, as the gloomy Egyptians believed) :—we will, even, say cannot *common-sense* conjure this phantom (for it is a phantom, as, out of this world, we can know nothing of it), until it really resolve itself into something that—so to express it—we can *shake-hands* with? Cannot this apparition, which makes our pleasant world uncomfortable for us, be laid? Cannot we—all we strong men—eject this terror of invisible *thinking* things—spectators of us—out of the world? Nothing is really done, until this be done. That is, if it can ever be done. Man is absolutely not really in his world, until this other thing is given notice to get out of it.

But, alas!—however desirable, however necessary to the solid *status* of man, and to explain the reason why he has been thus sent about the world to "walk upright—gifted with a mind, and the "front," to "face the stars"—this ejection of that fear to him cannot be.

And why, cannot be?

We will quietly tell you, reader. Because this *fear* lies buried in the truth of things, and is *interpenetrate* with them. Man's interest lies quite in the other way than in the believing of it. This dread of the supernatural is the clog upon his boldness;—the mistrust which spoils his plans;—which interferes with his prosperity;—which brings a cloud over the sunshine of his certainty. Man, then, when he begins to think, is afflicted with this fearful mistrust, that, after all, perhaps his very life may be the "dream," and that unknown future which is filled with those whom he knew, is the "waking." Where have our friends gone? They have disappeared as from out of the "ship" which has carried us, up to the present, and has left us only that "plain of silent, unanswering ocean;" upon which (and we still above it), to gaze, and to think.

Are there well-known faces about us, although we see them not? Are there "silent feet"—threading the passages of the world outside of our real world—though we see them not? And is it possible to come suddenly upon these—although it is not intended that we should come suddenly upon them;—and to hear that which it is not intended that we should hear. Is this sort of miracle, or "flash," possible in the (contrarily-struck) waves of spirit and body?

Now we would contend that man is much better—would be much happier—without all this unpleasant possibility. We would be understood to say that he must feel much more agreeably in his old familiar world—without spirit in it.

This is the real reason of the derision; this is the source of the affected pity at the belief of them; this is the cause of the indignation at them, which await all accounts of the marvellous. Men secretly tremble. But they are so boastful, so arrogant, so dreadfully afraid of the opinions of society (whatever that may mean), that they hide their fears, and bow to the real and the evident (that is the " real," and the " evident" of twelve o'clock at noon, and not twelve o'clock at midnight, under the supposed defiance, and in the boastful jest). In company they are bold. Separately they reflect, in their own secret minds, that, after all, these things may be true:—may be independent of newspapers, of popular talk, and of " critical reviews."

There is a distrust, in the thinking man's mind, that statements apparently supernatural may possibly be true (after all), on account of certain independent confirmatory surmises of his own; true from similar personal unaccountable experiences; or from the assurance of some friend whom the recipient is *disposed* to believe. But the recipient cannot be more than *disposed* to believe.

Modern times are only scientific. They evade questions that are not real. This modern cultured period is independent of superstition.

Superstition?—may be the echo of this theorem. Superstition, we can repeat, in the assurance that in the undercurrent of intelligence, now more than ever prevalent, there was perhaps never a time in the world fuller of SUPERSTITION. This quiet (apparently) modern time is full of it over and over again.

But, notwithstanding this firm reliance on, and belief of the *dicta* of science, and therefore of unfailing natural law, Man (and particularly Englishmen, spite of their quiet outside) ; the man has restless curiosity— man loves real truth, if he can obtain it—he solicits eagerly that which he can finally depend upon. He would believe if he could. But the evidence for supernatural things is so evasive—so fantastic—so, in one word, *unreliable*, that he will hold with that which he is told. And he is indoctrinated with science. " All mystery," the modern man says, " is that only partially known. When that which constitutes a thing is understood," the modern man declares, " the mystery ceases. He only finds nature." " Unknown nature" before—necessarily. Now " known nature' as "*proven* nature." Nature is the same "yesterday, to-day, and to-morrow."

"The highest example of a *person* we know any- thing about is a human person possessing but scanty knowledge and a frequently erring will, moving about in a very limited portion of space, and occupying at any one moment a portion infinitesimally small. But the GREAT FIRST CAUSE, as I conceive Him, fills all space, and is everything great and stupendous, and small and unknown and unnoticed (and is equally in existence the one with the other), and possesses attributes which supersede and infinitely transcend the mere human attributes of knowledge and will. But for these attributes we have no name. And I, for one, refuse to apply to them names which mean something vastly inferior, and possibly altogether different in their nature." Such are the views of a Modern Agnostic.

"Belief is passive:" he adds. "Faith is active. Belief rests on evidence derived from things seen. Faith explores the unseen, and discovers evidence where none was before found.

"Any one who has been in the habit of hearing sermons or reading theological works during the last forty years (which have proved revolutionary in regard to many things) can scarcely fail to have noticed the great change that has come over the religious world in that period.

"Forty years ago it was common to hear preachers and writers making assertions which implied a knowledge of heaven, of earth, and of hell, of past, present, and future, and for every assertion they made they were ready with a 'text of Scripture,' which they would quote by way of what they called *proof*. It never seems to have occurred to such, that there was a possibility of their misunderstanding or misapplying their quotations. But *now* we may observe a reticence of speech, a modesty of assertion, and an absence of false assurance, which are eminently characteristic of the Agnostic spirit. In this form Agnosticism has made its way into all our churches, and among all classes of religious men. Ridiculed, sneered-at, lampooned, misrepresented, and associated with the foulest epithets; without any recognised leader, and, till quite lately, without a distinctive name, it has, in view of its inherent vitality, permeated all creeds, while it is antagonistic to none."

A very noteworthy and encouraging proof of the general interest evoked in the present day amongst enquiring minds is afforded in the success, amidst liberal thinkers, of the writings of Arthur Schopenhauer. He was a truly remarkable man; and his ideas and conclusions, in regard to the main problems of life, are full of a very peculiar profundity. It is impossible to contradict any of his conclusions by any of the usual range of theosophical arguments. But at the same time his philosophy offers a very gloomy and discouraging, if, at the same time—as some think—it be a *true* prospect, of the complexities and the enigmas of life:—as man knows, and only can know, life.

The peculiarity of Schopenhauer's mental attitude may have had something to do with the tacit resolve of the university professors to *ignore* him, instead of refuting him. His principal work, "*Die Welt als Wille und Vorstellung*," was published in 1818, and was soon afterwards reviewed by Herbert; who called "Reinhold the First, Fichte the most profound, the most comprehensive; but Schopenhauer the most ingenious, and the *clearest* of all the philosophers."

It is not a little singular that the mystical philosophy of Schopenhauer ranges under the same head of philosophy, and, in its profundity, bespeaks the same, or (at least) a very similar insight into the real, underlying base or groundwork (apart from exemplification) of Buddhism. In witness of this unexpected proposition, we may adduce the following:—

"Knowledge, or perception, is an effect of the

objectivating will, blindly struggling, in the interests of self-preservation, towards what may help it to dominate material opposition; and with this intervention of will in the world of appearance, *the reign of Maja, illusion, begins.* Reason and error are twins. The analogies observable in nature are signs of the unity of 'will' in all the multiplicity of appearances which, side by side, fill the world of space, or elbow each other as successive incidents in time."

The real meaning of "will," as a word made use of by Schopenhauer, is in Hume or Berkeley's philosophy "power" or "force," *ab extra,* or "in itself."

"Will" is a product of "matter." "Matter" is a conception of the mind. The two are correlated, or rather they are the two sides of the same thing. The means of their union (although there must be such means) cannot be a subject of the thought or the imagination of man. This is, because there can be no *intellect* in "miracle." It is *Faith* alone which makes "miracle." Miracle is a denial of nature, because it denies the evidence of the senses. Miracle is impossible in reason. *Reason* must be laid down, when a conviction of *miracle* is taken up.

This conception of will is the corner-stone of Schopenhauer's philosophy. The unity of will is a deeply mystical doctrine. Schopenhauer does not attempt to demonstrate it. But even if it were conceded, there would still remain the latent antagonism between will as real and as intelligent, which makes it possible for him to propose that the self-denial of the one should neutralise the blind creative energy, the craving for life, of the other.

An intelligent modern author, in a review of Arthur Schopenhauer's works, comments thus—" Musical intuitions are an unconscious metaphysic, and, like the intuition of pure reason, cannot be translated into any language but that of direct perception. The analogy is close; although, of course, the language of one sense cannot be accepted as an equivalent for that of all. But the majority of men contemplate the Platonic ideas with which a person, without a musical ear, listens to a melody. Common-sense says that there must be a meaning in the balanced sounds; but, like the music of the spheres, it is couched in a language which the listener does not understand."

Schopenhauer draws a very ingenious parallel, and supplies a very apt illustration of the difference, and, at the same time, the identity of Free-Will and of Necessity—or the power to act either from within or from without. He supposes a man standing in the street, and thinking to himself—" It is six o'clock in the evening, and the day's work is ended. I can now go for a walk, or I can go to my club. I can also go up to the tower to see the sun set, or I can go to the theatre, or I can go to see this or the other friend. I can even go to the limits of the town, and pass on out into the country, and can even change my *locus-in-quo*, and the personality of the ' machine of the senses,' called ' myself'—and felt as ' *myself*'— going into the wilderness of scenes, and I may never come back again. *Never come back again!*— this is death to all visible purposes. Nevertheless I do none of these things. But still of my own (sup-posed) free-will I '*go straight home to my wife.*' This is just the same as if the water said—'I can make great waves (yes, in the bed of the stream, and, with a wider scope) in the mighty ocean. I can rush down headlong in foam and spray (yes, in a waterfall), or (in a grander and more stupendous realisation) like another Niagara, I can rise raylike into the air (yes, in a fountain). I can even boil away and disappear (yes, at eighty degrees of heat); yet I do none of all these possibilites,' quoth the water, 'but I remain (of my own free-will) clear and glassy in the tranquil lake—to be disturbed alone by the *reflections* into it. Just as, perhaps, life itself is only the *reflections* from the outside — or the *phantasmata*—of the Great Fashioner or Architect, building-up a *perceived* world, and amusing therewith (or beguiling) the creatures within it." What is all this but the *Nirvana* of the Buddhists? It is Buddhism.

Schopenhauer's philosophy, however far-reaching and deeply-searching, is melancholy—nay, despairing. In different places in his writings he has given expres-sion to the following opinions:—"The existence of the world is sin, and its essence misery. Each indi-vidual, on account of his being, is a partaker, as the heir of Adam, in the Grand Transgression, and there-fore fitly partakes in the suffering." Schopenhauer, indeed, might have argued, like one of his followers, *a non posse ad non esse.* "The cause of things in general," he says, "must be irrational, for how *could* such a preposterous concatenation of things have a *raison d'être?*" And the end must justify the means, if, rather than leave the whole creation without prospect of redemption, man sacrificed, in a despairing hope, that the will might yet, one day, learn wisdom enough to cease to perpetuate its own folly. For, to use the philosopher's own words, " this is as a rule the course of a man's life, that, ' *befooled by hope, he dances into the arms of death.*' He makes any effort towards the future only to *anticipate* his own pain. Mystics are generally pessimists, and as they see no end or limit in experience, they naturally despair—the generations taking up the weary tale of repetition, and only varying the forms. The unintelligent affirmation of will extends beyond the individual to the careful preservation of the species, which secret Nature holds secure to itself in the uncontrollable desire of the flesh, and in the exquisite mechanism of the body (male and female), all fashioned to the master-end of life—propagation. *Why* we know not, nor can we ever know. It is the poison of the world. The legend of the Fall of Man, in Genesis, is the one deep central truth in the Old Testament. Our fellow sufferers are to be pitied more than blamed. Man is a solecism—something that ought not to be at all; and what can be expected from creatures in such a predicament? The world resembles a penal colony, in which men of genius, like state criminals, suffer more than common offenders. Because the society of their inferiors is an additional pain, they therefore take refuge in solitude.

"If the world were not something which, in its practical expression, *ought not to be*, it would not be a theoretical riddle ; on the contrary, its existence would be either its own explanation, and that so self-evidently that it could occur to no one to ask for another, or else its purpose would be unmistakably recognisable.

" Pain, toil, and poverty," are the expressions of Schopenhauer; " these are the ballast which keep the human ship erect, which prevents its foundering in the deadly emptyness of a fool's paradise. This explains the mystical and Christian doctrine of the sanctifying effect of suffering. The individual shares, perforce, a world's load of pain, and then, if not before, recognises his solidarity in the whole sad lot of the universe. His will is paralysed by the discovery of its consequent impotence, and this sudden emancipation, its release from the slavery of motive and reason by a revelation of their radical and necessary insufficiency, is called, in religion, *grace*, and a *new birth*."

" The existence of Evil, whether physical or moral, is commonly thought of as a serious defect in the Divine government of the world; or at least an enigma which we must not impiously endeavour to solve. But approaching the *phenomenon* along the track we have chosen, it appears simply as a manifestation of superior creative energy, or of a process of *evolution* carried to a higher stage. A new faculty, or capacity, has been added to those which existed in any of the other forms of animal life. And how prodigious an advance this is over all other manifestations of the Unknowable is seen in the attitude assumed by Man in respect of other *phenomena*. It was no mere legend that ascribed to Man a likeness to the Gods when he partook of the 'Tree of Knowledge,' and acquired the power of distinguishing between 'Good and Evil.' In the exercise of this faculty, Man sat in judgment on the works of the Creator; on the manifestations of the 'Unknowable.' He did not dare, it is true, to declare the Creator the author of evil, but in calling him *good* he implied that it was a question which had to be settled, and to be settled by man's judgment. And yet there were many things in the world which appeared to be the work of a malignant being, or of malignant beings, rather than that of a kind and benignant Creator, and the anomaly was temporarily solved by ascribing these maleficent manifestations to wicked spirits, to demons, and finally to a personal devil—which means the shadows or the other side of nature. Mr. John Stuart Mill's famous arraignment of Nature may be quoted literally, as an exhibition of some of the modes in which the 'Unknowable' manifests itself."

Nothing, in a philosophical judgment, is more certain than that the presence of darkness is necessary to constitute light, and that, in the abstract sense, it is *light itself.* This was the persuasion of the world-old Egyptians, and is the problem of Nature, seeming so contradictory, testified-to in those stupendous monuments—the veritable puzzle of the ages—the Pyramids and the Sphynx. The whole of the architecture of Egypt is suffused (so to speak) with this puzzle. It has misled the antiquaries in the far greater proportion. It still bewilders them. It is for this reason that the Egyptologists have misread—or rather *have never read at all*—the hieroglyphics. The *phenomena* of "light," when narrowly considered, are nothing other (in as far as the *phenomena* are real in this mortal state of the senses) than the presented side of "darkness." For it is well known that conceivable light is darkness in itself. We mean, that to be anything at all, which operation is to come under the power of the senses, it must be material. Even light itself may be conceived as so intense, as to shut out every imaginable object, and thus to become its own contrary and contradiction, and to be really identical with darkness. It is "Lucifer," or the Light-Bringer (*Lux-fero*), or the "Morning Star," in this meaning, which is the means of production of the variety of objects of sense—in reality of ourselves, and therefore of *existence*. For it is philosophically admitted, that out of the brain of man, which is its maker, there can neither be such a world as we recognise as the world, nor can there be a possibility of it. This reflection and remembrance are the whole of the world.

In regard of the evils of this world, Mr. John Stuart Mill has the following remarks, treating of the mode in which this exterior "will" of Schopenhauer manifests itself:—

"In sober truth," he says, "nearly all the things which men are hanged or imprisoned for doing to one another, are Nature's every day performances. Killing, the most criminal act recognised by human laws, Nature does once to every being that lives; and in a large proportion of cases, after protracted tortures such as only the greatest monsters whom we read of ever purposely inflicted on their living fellow-creatures. If, by an arbitrary reservation, we refuse to account anything murder but what abridges a certain term supposed to be allotted to human life, Nature also does this to all but a small per-centage of lives, and does it in all the modes, violent or insidious, in which the worst human beings take the lives of one another. Nature impales men, breaks them as if on a wheel, casts them to be devoured by wild beasts, burns them to death, crushes them with stones like the first Christian martyr, starves them with hunger, freezes them with cold, poisons them by the quick or slow venom of her exhalations, such as the ingenious cruelty of a Nero or a Domitian never surpassed. All this Nature does with the most supercilious disregard both of mercy and of justice, emptying her shafts upon the best and noblest indifferently with the meanest and worst; upon those who are engaged in the highest and worthiest enterprises, and often as the direct consequence of the noblest acts; and it might almost be imagined as a punishment for them. She mows down those on whose existence hangs the well-being of a whole people, perhaps the prospects of the human race for generations to come, with as little compunction as those whose death is a relief to themselves or a blessing to those under their noxious influence. Such are Nature's dealings with life. Even when she does not intend to kill, she inflicts the same tortures in apparent wantonness. In the clumsy provision which she has made for the perpetual renewal of criminal life rendered necessary by the prompt termination she puts to it in every individual instance, no human being ever comes into the world but another human being is literally stretched on the rack for hours or days, not infrequently issuing in death. Next to taking life (equal to it, according to high authority), is taking the means by which we live; and Nature does this too on the largest scale and with the most callous indifference. A single hurricane destroys the hopes of a season; a flight of locusts, or an inundation, desolates a district; a trifling chemical change in an edible root starves a million of people. The waves of the sea, like banditti, seize and appropriate the wealth of the rich and the little all of the poor with the same accompaniments of stripping, wounding, and killing as their human antitypes. Everything, in short, which the worst men commit either against life or property is perpetrated on a larger scale by natural agents. Nature has Noyades more fatal than those of Carrier; her explosions of fire-damp are as destructive as human artillery; her plague and cholera far surpass the poison cups of the Borgias. Even the love of 'order,' which is thought to be a following of the ways of Nature, is in fact a contradiction of them. All which people are accustomed to deprecate as 'disorder,' and its consequences is precisely a counterpart of Nature's ways. Anarchy and the Reign of Terror are overmatched in injustice, ruin, and death, by a hurricane and a pestilence." (*J. S. Mill, Essays on Religion.*)

If it is discredited by writers, the supernatural should not be treated-of by them. There are plenty of subjects at which they may play, but that—if they believe in the possibility of any life but their ordinary life—this so serious one. All that regards this most important subject—is *serious.* If the possibility of the supernatural be believed, and if any of its incidents be accepted, men are bound, as candid individuals and as honest individuals, to make the avowal that they believe. The explanations which are frequently offered of things appearing as supernatural are greatly more difficult to credit than the extra-natural (and supposed impossible) matters themselves. When examined closely, these elucidations often prove infinitely clumsy. Somewhat roughly looked-into, they continually fall to pieces of themselves. Nobody, in fact, credits the explanations of some unaccountable things. The un-comfortable fact, when " stared-at and queried" in daylight, is simply *got-rid of.* It is always considered *mal-apropos.* The subject is dismissed, to make way for the next-soliciting object. The wonder i. given-up as unexplainable. And this, in truth, is the whole process. This is a very easy, though not a very con-clusive or satisfactory method of disproving. We *suppose* we disbelieve. That is all.

It is impossible to confess or to imagine that the partitions between " This World" and the " Other World" are so thin, that you can hear the movers in the other through. This is the great objection of the world at large to the class of people denominated Spiritualists, because their assumptions are so entirely against common-sense ; and common-sense, as we receive common-sense, is the only basis upon which the whole world relies, and without which we can do nothing, nor can we be anything. The above states the whole case as between the world philoso-phical and the Spiritualists, contracted into a few words.

We are conscientious enemies to all those *pheno-*

mena ranged under the vague—very unmeaning—head of Spiritual Manifestations. We think that the use of this term has produced infinite harm in bringing discredit upon, and in vulgarising the general subject of, supernaturalism, and in misleading people's mind. We are weary of the jargon whereby strange and unexplainable—even possibly natural—doubtless, in the common-sense view, *natural—phenomena* have been degraded. The history of all unknown things has been thus similar, that at the outset they have invariably been invested with the attributes of the magical. We must carefully guard ourselves from credulity. Such things as these presumed Spiritual Disclosures have been known in all ages. They underlie and are the support of much that has been given us in the Bible narrative. And therefore they have been questioned as naturally unbelievable.

There is nothing newer other than that they have been suddenly and widely noticed in these psycho-logically-magnetic displays—this supposed spiritual betrayal, as issuing out of the "breaks of nature," so to express it—this counter-working and false-working of the universal sympathy and antipathy, or transitive evolvement—these aberrations of polarity. We have an abiding dislike to, and we cordially dissent from, all this epileptic wandering—all this convulsive, inco-herent, blameworthy—nay, *audacious* reaching-out for forbidden things. The pampered human mind—which is a notorious fact—can run into any extreme. We, on the contrary, are friends to the solidest and plainest common-sense. This is (in conclusion) as the rudder by which to guide the world. "Order is heaven's first law," because, unless number "Two" succeed to number " One," number " One" is impossible, inasmuch as it would be the whole " round of number" contained in " itself."   All this is, of course, purely " abstract and metaphysical."

THE END.

INDEX.

A.

Abury, 144.

Argonauts, The, 179.

Alchemists, The, 89.

All men are children in a certain sense, 102.

Analogy of the expansive natural characteristics of man to the growth of plants, 105.

Atheism impossible, 89.

B.

Baptism by water, its meaning, 121.

Baptism by Fire, or by the "Holy Spirit," 121.

Bacchus (Taurus), 170.

"Bahúmid," "Bafomet," 146.

Beauséant, or Templar banner, (mystical), 148.

Berkeley, Bishop, 2.

Brahmanic Worship, 6.

Brahmanism and Transcendental Philosophy, 21.

Buddhism and the Fire Philosophy, 27.

Buddhism and its abstract meaning, 27.

Buddhism—definition of, 1.

Buddhism, the foundation of all the religions of India, 1.

Buddhistic Philosophy of Life, 40.

C.

Castes, 9.

Cause and effect—philosophical and abstract, 2.

Ceremonies of the First of May, 165.

Chapter-Houses of the Cathedrals, 144.

Christian Trinity, abstract views regarding, 41.

Colours, phenomena of, 23.

Clement, Pope, 161.

Crook, The crook to the nave of a Cathedral analogous to the crook of the Bishop's *pedum*, 144.

D.

Divine destruction, 207.

Dreams are as the contradiction, and as the ill-adjustment (not regulated by the waking will, or logical propriety), and the ill-adjustment of the "freed" sections of the connecting reason, 98.

Dreams are as the natural ill-adjusted optic-glass of the soul, 98.

Dreams are as the contradiction, and the ill-adaptation of the presented sections of the liberated reason, 98.

Dreams, misunderstood and undervalued, 98.

Dreams, prophetic dreams possible, 98.

Dreams, deal with the most absurd contradictions, and the most trivial objects, 98.

Printed by Jas. Wade, 18, Tavistock-street, Covent-garden ,W.C.

ERRATA.

Page 7 (line 16), *for* "Gaza," *read* "Gaya."

  ,,   12 (line 12), *for* "matters," *read* "matter."

  ,,   36 (line 3), *for* "worn," *read* "won."

  ,,   38 (line 21), *for* "dress," *read* "dregs."

  ,,   38 (line 24), *for* "unto," *read* "into."

  ,,   42 (line 29), *for* "constructive," *read* "constrictive."

  ,,   48 (line 1), *for* "our example," *read* "one example."

  ,,   48 (line 18), *dele* "s" in "Schopenhauser."

  ,,   101 (line 16), *dele* "s" in "deaths."

  ,,   103 (line 4), *for* "their," *read* "there."

Mr. Redway's Publications.

Just Published, crown 8vo, cloth, price 4s. 6d.

Paul of Tarsus.

BY THE AUTHOR OF "RABBI JESHUA."

"Those who have read 'Rabbi Jeshua' will know what to expect in 'Paul of Tarsus,' from the pen of the same anonymous author. The work is most readable, though it is not all like the popular biographies of the Apostle which appear in so great numbers. The authors of these are generally careful to show their erudition. The author of this work seems to be careful to hide his, great and evident though it be. The justice of its local colour throughout, and the vividness of the pictures of Jerusalem, Antioch, and Rome, bespeak a scholar; while the charming style of the work, its simplicity and directness, show a writer of no mean literary skill."—*Scotsman.*

"A remarkable book. . . . The author has realised in his own mind a picture of Paul which, whether true or false, is vivid, and this he has reproduced in a style of unusual brilliance and power."—*Manchester Guardian.*

"The author has knowledge, imagination, and marked literary facility, and the result of these combined gifts is found in sketches which are rich in light, colour, life, and picturesqueness."—*Manchester Examiner.*

"Among those strange people who regard 'Robert Elsmere' as embodying in an attractive form the main teachings of Christianity 'Paul of Tarsus' may find favour for its merely literary excellence, which is undeniable."—*Morning Post.*

"A considerable sensation was created seven or eight years ago by the publication of 'Rabbi Jeshua,' a brilliant rhetorical study of the life of Jesus by one who regarded him as no Messiah, but as a pure-minded and high-souled enthusiast. The anonymous author now comes forward with a similar study. He fairly warns those 'whose hearts are firmly fixed in the lessons of their childhood,' and 'pious souls' who do not want their faith disturbed, to stop at the preface. . . . The great value of the work lies in its wonderfully vivid pictures of the social, religious, and political life of the times—pictures composed of skilfully grouped hints derived from a wide reading of contemporary, classical, and Talmudic literature."—*Christian World.*

GEORGE REDWAY, YORK STREET, COVENT GARDEN.

Crown 8vo, cloth, price 7s. 6d.

Theosophy, Religion, and Occult Science.

By HENRY S. OLCOTT,

President of the Theosophical Society.

WITH GLOSSARY OF EASTERN WORDS.

CONTENTS :—Theosophy or Materialism—Which ? — The Theosophical Society and its Aims—The Common Foundation of all Religions—Theosophy : the Scientific Basis of Religion—Theosophy : its Friends and Enemies—The Occult Sciences—Spiritualism and Theosophy—India : Past, Present, and Future—The Civilisation that India needs—The Spirit of the Zoroastrian Religion—The Life of Buddha and its Lessons, &c.

The *Manchester Examiner* describes these lectures as "RICH IN INTEREST AND SUGGESTIVENESS," and says that "the theosophy expounded in this volume is at once a theology, a metaphysic, and a sociology," and concludes a lengthy notice by stating that "Colonel Olcott's volume deserves, and will repay, the study of all readers for whom the byways of speculation have an irresistible charm."

GEORGE REDWAY, YORK STREET, COVENT GARDEN.

Nearly 500 pages, demy 8vo, cloth, price 18s.

The Development of Marriage and Kinship.

By C. STANILAND WAKE.

CONTENTS :—Preface. Introduction—Sexual Morality. Chapter I. Primeval Man. II. Supposed Promiscuity. III. Primitive Law of Marriage. IV. Group Marriage. V. Polyandry. VI. Polygyny. VII. Monandry. VIII. The Rule of Descent. IX. Kinship through Females. X. Kinship through Males. XI. Marriage by Capture. XII. Monogamy,

"The volume is a closely reasoned argument on a complicated and interesting subject, and will add to the reputation Mr. Wake has already earned by his writings on anthropology. It is easier reading than some earlier books on the same subject. . . . Mr. Wake concludes his study of these difficult but interesting questions by a chapter on modern civilised systems of monogamy and on Christian ideas relating to marriage and celibacy."—*Athenæum.*

"A fund of valuable information in regard to savage usages all over the world. . . . Mr. Wake gives a useful summary of the valuable investigation conducted by Mr. Lorimer Fison and Mr. Howitt into the Australian system of group marriage."—*Literary World.*

"Regarded as a mere storehouse of curious information as to the marriage customs which have at different times prevailed among different races there is a great deal which is interesting in the volume before us."—*John Bull.*

GEORGE REDWAY, YORK STREET, COVENT GARDEN.

Crown 8vo, cloth, price 7s 6d.

Posthumous Humanity:

A Study of Phantoms.

By ADOLPHE D'ASSIER,

Member of the Bordeaux Academy of Science.

TRANSLATED AND ANNOTATED BY HENRY S. OLCOTT, PRESIDENT OF THE
THEOSOPHICAL SOCIETY.

CONTENTS :—Facts Establishing the Existence of the Posthumous Personality in Man—Its Various Modes of Manifestation—Facts Establishing the Existence of a Second Personality in the Living Man—Its Various Modes of Manifestation—Facts Establishing the Existence of the Personality in Animals, and concerning a Posthumous Animality—Fluidic Form of Vegetables—Fluidic Form of Gross Bodies—Character of the Posthumous Being—Its Physical Constitution—Its Aversion to Light—Its Reservoir of Living Force—Its Ballistic—The Nervous Fluid—Electric Animals—Electric Persons—Electric Plants—The Mesmeric Ether and the Personality which it Engenders—The Somnambule—The Sleep-talker—The Seer—The Turning-table—The Talking-table—The Medium—Miracles of the Ecstatics—Prodigy of Magic—The Incubus—The Obsessing Spirit—Causes of the Rarity of the Living Phantom—Causes of the Rarity of the Trans-sepulchral Phantom—Resemblance of the Spiritistic Phenomena to the Phenomena of the Posthumous Order—Lycanthropy—Glance at the Fauna of the Shades—Their Pre-occupations—How they Prolong their Existence—The Posthumous Vampire.

Truth says:—"If you care for GHOST STORIES, DULY ACCREDITED, EXCELLENTLY TOLD, AND SCIENTIFICALLY EXPLAINED, you should read the translation by Colonel Olcott of M. Adolphe d'Assier's 'Posthumous Humanity,' a study of phantoms. There is no dogmatism so dogged and offensive as that of the professed sceptic—of the scientific sceptic especially—who *ex vi termini* ought to keep the doors of his mind hospitably open; and it is refreshing, therefore, to find such scientists as Wallace, Crookes, and M. d'Assier, who is a Positivist, in the ranks of the Psychical Research host. For my own part, though I have attended the seance of a celebrated London medium, and there convinced myself beyond all doubt of his imposture, I no more think that the detection of a medium fraud disposes of the whole question of ghosts, &c., than that the detection of an atheist priest disposes of the whole question of Christianity. Whatever view you take of this controversy, however, I can promise you that you will find the book interesting at least if not convincing."

GEORGE REDWAY, YORK STREET, COVENT GARDEN.

315 pages, demy 8vo, cloth, price 10s. 6d.

Lives of Alchemystical Philosophers.

BASED ON MATERIALS COLLECTED IN 1815, AND SUPPLEMENTED BY RECENT RESEARCHES.

WITH A PHILOSOPHICAL DEMONSTRATION OF THE TRUE PRINCIPLES OF THE MAGNUM OPUS, OR GREAT WORK OF ALCHEMICAL RE-CONSTRUCTION, AND SOME ACCOUNT OF THE SPIRITUAL CHEMISTRY.

By ARTHUR EDWARD WAITE.

TO WHICH IS ADDED A BIBLIOGRAPHY OF ALCHEMY AND HERMETIC PHILOSOPHY.

LIVES OF THE ALCHEMISTS:—Geber—Rhasis—Alfarabi—Avicenna—Morien—Albertus Magnus—Thomas Aquinas—Roger Bacon—Alain of Lisle—Raymond Lully—Arnold De Villanova—Jean De Meung—The Monk Ferarius—Pope John XXII.—Nicholas Flamel—Peter Bono—Johannes De Rupecissa—Basil Valentine—Isaac of Holland—Bernard Trévisan—John Fontaine—Thomas Norton—Thomas Dalton—Sir George Ripley—Picus De Mirandola—Paracelsus—Denis Zachaire—Berigard of Pisa—Thomas Charnock—(Giovanni Braccesco—Leonardi Fioravanti—John Dee—Henry Khunrath—Michael Maier—Jacob Böhme—J. B. Van Helmont—Butler—Jean D'Espagnet—Alexander Sethon—Michael Sendivogius—Gustenbover—Busardier—Anonymous Adept—Albert Belin—Eirenæus Philalethes—Pierre Jean Fabre—John Frederick Helvetius—Guiseppe Francesco Borri—John Heydon—Lascaris—Delisle—John Hermann Obereit—Travels, Adventures, and Imprisonments of Joseph Balsamo.

"The biographical sketches of the alchemists, both true and false, are curious reading, and the alphabetical catalogue of works on Hermetic Philosophy is surprisingly suggestive of ages when leisure was less scarce, and literature scarcer, than in modern days."—*Daily News.*

---

612 pages, large 8vo, WITH PLATES, *price 15s.*

The Hidden Way Across the Threshold;

OR,

The Mystery which hath been Hidden for Ages and from Generations.

An Explanation of the CONCEALED FORCES IN EVERY MAN to open the Temple of the Soul, and to learn the guidance of the Unseen Hand.

ILLUSTRATED AND MADE PLAIN WITH AS FEW OCCULT PHRASES AS POSSIBLE,

By J. C. STREET.

www.ingramcontent.com/pod-product-compliance
Lightning Source LLC
Chambersburg PA
CBHW060607030726
47498CB00005B/1583